INSIDE
TEXTBOOKS

WHAT STUDENTS NEED TO KNOW

Thomas W. Adams
University of Pennsylvania

ADDISON-WESLEY PUBLISHING COMPANY
Reading, Massachusetts • Menlo Park, California • New York
Don Mills, Ontario • Wokingham, England • Amsterdam
Sydney • Bonn • Singapore • Tokyo • Madrid • San Juan

A Publication of the World Language Division

Sponsoring Editor: Kathleen Sands-Boehmer
Developmental Editor: Talbot F. Hamlin
Production/Manufacturing: James W. Gibbons

Text design by Herb Caswell
Cover design by Jean Seal

ISBN 0-201-10699-X
2 3 4 5 6 7 8 9 10 11-AL-96 95 94 93 92 91

Preface to the Instructor

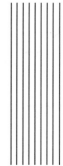

Why a Textbook About Textbooks?

Limited English Proficient (LEP) students are not unacquainted with textbooks, since they have used texts in their English language classes. But in approach and design, virtually all ESL/EFL books differ in significant ways from content-area texts used in English-medium schools and universities. This observation suggests that these students will face a beast they are ill-equipped to do battle with — the school or university textbook.

This beast is awesome indeed. In order to be mastered, it must be understood conceptually, linguistically, and organizationally. Clearly, the first falls outside the scope of an ESL book. We cannot possibly cover the basics of subjects ranging from quantum physics to abnormal psychology.

What we can do, however, is examine the language and organization of textbooks. Conceptual content aside, most textbooks are surprisingly similar in approach and appearance. Students familiar with the style of academic writing and aware of organizational conventions will find the beast much less formidable.

Who Should Use This Text?

Inside Textbooks is intended for use by students planning to enter secondary schools and universities throughout the world where the course textbooks will be in English.

Language Level

Inside Textbooks can effectively be used by students having a high intermediate-level competency in English corresponding roughly to a minimum TOEFL score of 450.

Background and Rationale of *Inside Textbooks*

This book was written in Saudi Arabia. For seven years, I taught there at a technical university where English is the medium of instruction and where the textbooks assigned to undergraduates were the same ones assigned to their North American counterparts. Studying from a textbook can be a daunting experience for any student: for ours, it was particularly so.

Because few ESL/EFL texts addressed this situation and even fewer were appropriate for our students, I decided to give it a go. *Inside Textbooks* is the result.

Two irreconcilable schools of thought competed for the form the book might take. One holds that students learn by doing. The other maintains that students learn by analyzing and then doing. The first school, for example, would contend that no manual can teach a student how to drive: only the experience can. The opposing view holds that no manual can replace the experience, but it can pave the way for the experience. As applied to this project, the first school would endorse a reader. The second would call for a manual.

I chose the latter. A decision to compile a reader would have resulted in the exclusion of many teaching points I wanted to address. A decision to devise a manual, however, would in no way preclude the use of companion readings. An attempt to wed the two views would double the length of this book.

The form now set, an identification of possible content followed. As virtually none of my students could claim familiarity with textbooks used in North America, major problems associated with reading them quickly became apparent. This part of my task was mercifully easy.

Deciding on exactly what to include was not. I did not want *Inside Textbooks* to be yet another extended exercise in skimming, scanning, and locating main ideas. Because a great number of ESL/EFL texts emphasize these key reading strategies, I felt my efforts might better be directed toward an examination of reading problems frequently not addressed elsewhere.

Suggested Use

Instructors will find that *Inside Textbooks* can easily be adapted to their own or their students' needs. The text works particularly well in small group settings or when used wholly as out-of-class assignments. Although the chapters follow a logical order, they need not be assigned sequentially nor need they all be covered.

If students are not taking content-area courses concurrent to studying *Inside*, instructors may wish to assign readings from various textbooks. Twenty passages to be used as points of departure for such assignments are included in Appendix B.

Acknowledgments

Addison-Wesley provided a number of anonymous reviewers whose criticisms prompted changes both great and small. Another debt of gratitude is owed colleagues and friends who advertently or otherwise aided in this project. I am pleased to acknowledge them here:

Richard Albertson
University of Petroleum & Minerals

Martin Drury
University of Petroleum & Minerals

Susan Kuder
Northeastern University

Bea Mikulecky
Boston University

Mohammed A. Mulla
University of Petroleum & Minerals

Maryann O'Brien
University of Houston

William Phillips
University of Petroleum & Minerals

David Scheller
ARAMCO; Dhahran, Saudi Arabia

A heartfelt expression of thanks to Addison Wesley's acquisition editor, Kathy Sands-Boehmer, who from the conception of this project in 1986 through its completion gently urged many changes. I am fortunate to have worked with Tab Hamlin, my developmental editor, whose expertise over many years in editing textbooks in a variety of subject areas was indispensable in the preparation of *Inside Textbooks*.

Students at the University of Petroleum & Minerals and the University of Pennsylvania participated in classroom trials of these materials.

Credits

Passage 19 in Appendix B is based upon an article written by T.W. Adams which first appeared in the January 1987 issue of *English Today*, a publication of Cambridge University Press.

Contents

Introduction to the Student

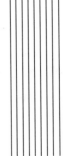

This book will not teach you the fundamentals of organic chemistry or the principles of molecular biology. That is the function of textbooks in these subjects. But to understand the textbooks in these and other areas, you first need to know how textbooks are organized and how to read them effectively. This book will help.

If you are using this book in class, your teacher will give you instructions on how to use it to your best advantage. If, however, you are studying this book without the help of a teacher, you will be wise to start with the first chapter and work your way through each page until you finish the book.

As you study this book, try to develop the habits that you will need in order to read efficiently. These habits are described in the next few paragraphs.

Habit 1: Sample your textbook.

The first time you pick up your textbook, take a few minutes to see how it is organized and what it contains. Look at the sections in the front and the back. Then examine a few of the chapters to see how they are organized. If you have an adequate overview of your textbook, you will understand your reading assignments better.

Habit 2: Preview your assignments.

Do not begin with a close, careful reading of the entire assignment. Instead, quickly look over the entire reading page by page, paying particular attention to the titles of various sections and to the first and last sentence of each paragraph. Also examine illustrations and any other information that will help give you a broad, general view of the central ideas of the reading. By doing this, you will not only have an idea of the content of the reading, you will also see how the reading is organized. You should spend only a few minutes previewing your assignment.

Habit 3: Organize your study time.

Keep in mind the number of pages in your assignments and then estimate how long it will take you to read them. If you know that you have quite a few pages to read before your next class, make sure that you have put aside enough time. Try to find enough time to finish the assignment from one textbook before you begin reading an assignment from a different textbook.

Habit 4: Vary your reading speed.

How fast you read will depend on how easy or difficult your assignment is. Even within a particular passage, some parts will be easier to read than others. Good readers will vary their speed according to how difficult or easy a passage is.

Habit 5: Reread if necessary.

The information in your textbooks builds upon itself. This means that you will need to have a fairly good understanding of the content of earlier assignments in order to understand the content of later ones. If you find that you understand very little of your assignment, try reading it again. Even native speakers sometimes reread their assignments several times before they understand the content well.

Habit 6: Make use of previous knowledge.

Relate the information in your textbooks to experiences from your own life, to your previous knowledge of the subject you are reading, and to the subjects you are studying in your other classes. By making these connections or associations, you will make your readings more meaningful.

Habit 7: Mark key information.

Not all sentences and paragraphs are equally important. Good readers are able to separate the important from the unimportant. When you come across key statements, identify them in some way. If the textbook you are studying belongs to you, you can do this by underlining or highlighting these key statements directly in your textbook. Alternatively, you can call attention to important ideas by drawing arrows or stars next to them. If the textbook does not belong to you, you can record key information in a notebook or on index cards. This practice will help when you review your assignments at a later time.

Habit 8: Interact with the author.

Try to turn your reading assignments into dialogs with the author. Question and challenge the author. Analyze and evaluate the content of your assignments. By taking an active role when you read, you will find that your understanding of assignments will increase.

In the following chapters, you will learn more about these habits.

CHAPTER 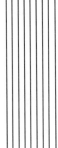1

Between the Covers

Study Objectives

By the end of this chapter, you should be able to:

- locate and use the various sections found in the front of and back of textbooks.

Imagine that today is the beginning of the school year. You have registered for class and collected your texts from the bookstore. What next? There is no need to wait until your first class before opening a book. In fact, now is the best time to look inside your textbooks.

Each of your texts has many different sections, or parts. In this chapter, we will look at these sections. Not every book has every section, but most of them are found in most books.

1.1   Title

A surprising amount of information can be learned about a book by examining its title. Look at the following title: *Physics for Biology and Pre-medical Students*. The word "physics" indicates that this is a study of the science that deals with the properties, changes, and interactions of matter and energy. The book is intended for people who are principally interested in the study of living organisms. The words "for biology and pre-medical students" tell us so. The title indicates the subject and the audience for the book. A title can also tell other things about a book. The title, *A First Course in Calculus*, tells you that the book is for students who have not

1

> **A Successful Text**
>
> In 1948, Professor Paul Samuelson published his classic textbook called *Economics*. Every three or four years, Samuelson updates his book to reflect recent developments in the field. In 1987, his text was in its 12th edition. To date, more than four million copies have been sold.

previously studied calculus. It is a beginning book in that subject. The word "course" tells you that the book contains a program of instruction. It is a textbook, not a reference book. This title indicates the level and the type of book as well as the subject.

Now read the following title. Then fill in the blanks about it.

Basic Statistics for Business Majors: 3rd ed.

subject: _____

audience: _____

level: _____

If you look back at the title of the statistics book, you will notice that it includes the words "3rd ed." This is an abbreviation for "third edition." Every several years, a new version (edition) of the same textbook appears on the market. Textbooks are changed from time to time so that the latest information can be included in them. If the title of a book does not mention its edition, then the book is probably in its first edition. Look again at the title on the cover of this textbook.

What edition do you think it is?

edition number: _____

1.2   Author

The next step is to ask who wrote the textbook. This can be answered by having a look at one of the first pages of the book. This is called the title page. On it you will find the following information:

(1) the title of the book;
(2) the name of the author; and often
(3) the name of the college or university where the author teaches.

Additional information about the author can sometimes be found in a section located either on the back cover of the book or on a page somewhere in the front. You may feel better about reading a textbook if you know something about its author. Find the section which gives information about the author of this book. Put a checkmark below to show where it is located.

_____ front pages   _____ back cover

1.3   Table of Contents

At the beginning of every book you will find a page or two that lists the major sections or divisions of the textbook. This list is called the **table of contents** or simply **contents**. Here you can find an outline of what the book contains and the number of the page which begins each section.

An examination of the table of contents will show how topics are developed. Textbooks are usually organized in one of two ways.

1. Chronologically — This approach arranges the topics according to their appearance in the history of the subject.

2. Conceptually — This approach arranges topics according to general ideas or notions. Basic, fundamental ideas and principles are discussed first, and complex ones later.

Decide which one of the following two types of textbooks is likely to be arranged chronologically, and which one is likely to be arranged conceptually:

_____ history   _____ biology

Go to the table of contents in this textbook and decide which approach is used. Use a checkmark to indicate your answer.

_____ conceptual   _____ chronological

_____ combination

1.4   Preface, Foreword, and Introduction

A textbook sometimes begins with a section called a **preface, foreword**, or **introduction** that gives you information about that textbook. This information might explain how the textbook is organized and how to study it. A preface, foreword, or introduction might also identify the textbook's purpose and value. Some textbooks — including this one — have several sections. In this book, one section is directed toward teachers and the other section is for you. Look at the beginning of this book and fill in the following blanks.

Name of section for teachers: _____

Name of section for students: _____

The pages of the preface, foreword, or introduction are usually given Roman numerals. Arabic numerals are used beginning with the first chapter. Pages on the right have odd numbers, while pages on the left have even numbers.

Arabic:	1	2	3	4	5	6	7	8	9	10
Roman:	i	ii	iii	iv	v	vi	vii	viii	ix	x

Write the Arabic equivalents of the following Roman numbers.

xi = _____   xvii = _____

xv = _____   xxiv = _____

Turn to the last page of the preface in this book. Convert the Roman number on it into an Arabic numeral:

Arabic equivalent _____

1.5   Appendix

The **appendix** is located at the back of a textbook. This section contains material which supports or supplements information presented in the textbook. By pushing detailed information or extra exercises to the back of the text, an author can keep to the essential points within the textbook itself.

Turn to the appendixes in this book and decide whether they contain detailed information or extra exercises.

Appendix A: _____

Appendix B: _____

1.6   Glossary

The **glossary** is found at the back of the textbook. A glossary defines technical words that are used in the textbook. Turn to the glossary of this book and answer the following questions.

How are words in the glossary arranged?

_____ alphabetically   _____ in the order they are presented
in the textbook

Does the glossary give the page number(s) where these words are used in the textbook?

_____ yes   _____ no

1.7   References

When information from one publication (e.g., a book or journal) is used in another publication, the source of that information is included in a list that is alphabetized according to the family name of its author. This list is called the **references**.

A textbook either has one comprehensive list of references located near the back of the book or many smaller lists located at the end of each chapter. Where can references be found in this book?

_____ back of book   _____ end of chapters

You will know when an author refers to other publications because a special note is used. There are several kinds of notes. One note is enclosed in parentheses and includes the family name of the writer of the other publication and the year the publication was printed. An example of this kind of note can be found in the second paragraph of the first page of Chapter 3.

What is the author's name? _____

What year was the publication printed? _____

Now turn to the first paragraph of Chapter 4. You will notice that only the year is enclosed in parentheses. The author's name appears elsewhere in the same sentence.

What is the author's name? _____

What year was the publication printed? _____

Go to the references in order to find complete information about these publications.

name of publication in Chapter 3: _____

name of publication in Chapter 4: _____

1.8   Answer Key

Some textbooks include a section that provides answers to problems or exercises. The author may include all answers or may only supply the answers to even or odd questions. Find the answer key in this text and put a checkmark on the appropriate line below.

_____ answers to even   _____ answers to odd
questions only   questions only

_____ all answers given   _____ no answers given

1.9   Index

The final section of most textbooks is called the **index**. The index is an alphabetical listing of important items which are discussed in the text. Each item in the index is called an **entry**. Entries include the names of people, as well as words, terms, and concepts. Find the first and last entry in the index of this book and write them here:

first entry: _____

last entry: _____

In some textbooks, there are two indexes: one for general concepts (often called a subject index) and one for the names of people or places. Names of people are entered according to family name, as in:

Kuder, Susan R.

family name _____↑   ↑_____ first name and
middle initial

Write the name of the author of this textbook as it would appear in an index:

_____

Go to the back of this book to see which indexes are included. Use checkmarks for your answers.

_____ subject index   _____ name index

_____ general index

Each entry in an index is followed by page numbers or section numbers (see Section 2.2). These numbers show where an idea is discussed in the book. Look in the index of this book to see if page or section numbers are used. Answer with a checkmark.

_____ page numbers   _____ section numbers

On the first page of an index, you may find a note that explains its system of organization. Find the note in this book and answer the following questions:

What does boldfaced type indicate? _____

What does "f" represent? _____

What does "t" indicate? _____

When searching the index for a particular entry, you should be prepared to look in several places. For instance, another chapter in this book discusses various types of words that express judgments. This topic will be entered into the index in one or even in several different ways. Four possibilities are listed below. Check the index to see how this topic is listed.

_____ Types of judgments   _____ Judgmental language

_____ Language, judgmental   _____ Words, types of

You can see that although a topic may be listed in several places, it may not be listed in the way that you think it will. If you cannot find your topic immediately, think of other ways the author might list it.

Summary

In this chapter, you studied several steps to follow when examining a textbook for the first time. These steps can be summarized as follows.

1. Examine the title.
2. Locate information about the author.
3. Open the book to the table of contents and study it to see what materials are included and whether they are presented chronologically or conceptually.
4. Have a look at the preface, foreword, or introduction.
5. Check the back of the book to see what supplementary sections are included.

Key Vocabulary

appendix	glossary	references
author	index	table of contents
entry	preface	title page

Recommended Reading

Bradley, Anne. 1983. *Take Note of College Study Skills*. Glenview, IL: Scott, Foresman. See Chapter 8 on textbook parts.

Kimmelman, Joan et al. 1984. *Reading and Study Skills*. New York: Macmillan. See Chapter 5 on previewing.

Thought Questions

1. In what way can a table of contents be compared to a skeleton?

2. What kinds of information would most likely be found in the appendix of a mathematics textbook? a chemistry textbook? a business textbook?

3. Explain how a table of contents is organized differently from an index.

4. In what ways are glossaries similar to dictionaries? In what ways are they different?

5. Suggest several other titles for this textbook.

6. Look at one of your textbooks. Number the following according to their order of appearance in that textbook.

____ acknowledgments   ____ glossary

____ answer key   ____ index

____ appendix   ____ preface

____ bibliography   ____ table of contents

____ title page

7. Find the plural spellings for index and appendix in a dictionary. Both words have two plural forms. Write them here.

index _____   _____

appendix _____   _____

Exercises

Exercise A Examine the titles of the textbooks below. Put a checkmark in the appropriate column if the level or audience can be determined.

	Level	Audience	Title
1.	___	___	Intermediate Oceanography
2.	___	___	Statistics for Engineers
3.	___	___	Business Fundamentals
4.	___	___	Office Correspondence
5.	___	___	Anthropology: A Notional View
6.	___	___	Psychology for Teachers
7.	___	___	Advanced Urban Geography
8.	___	___	Introducing American Literature
9.	___	___	Sociology: A Cognitive Approach
10.	___	___	Logic: The Basics

Exercise B   Examine the following extracts from various tables of contents and decide if they are organized conceptually or chronologically.

1. _____

THE NATURE OF AMERICAN BUSINESS
   The U.S. Business System
   Business in America
   Capitalism
   Improving the Standard of Living

2. _____

THE EARTH
   Ancient Civilizations
   The Dark Ages
   The Age of Discovery

3. _____

WATER
   Molecules
   Physical Properties of Water
   Solvent Properties of Water

4. _____

HUMAN CIVILIZATION
   Europe
   The Near East
   Southeast Asia
   Africa

5. _____

UNITED STATES COMMERCIAL POLICY
   The Trade Agreements Act of 1934
   General Agreement on Tariffs and
      Trade
   The 1962 Trade Expansion Act
   The Trade Reform Act of 1974

6. _____

THE HUMAN POPULATION
   Dynamics of Population Growth
   Nature's Checks on Growth
   World Population Growth
   Problems of Overpopulation

7. _____

MONEY AND ITS CREATION
   Bartering: The Oldest System of
      Trading
   The First Banks
   Computerized Banking

8. _____

THE COMING OF THE INDUSTRIAL AGE
   The Roots of Modern Industrialism
   Rise of the Factory System
   The Steam Engine
   The Railway Age

9. _____

COMPUTERS IN ARCHITECTURE
   Graphic Design
   Applications
   Careers

10. _____

PHYSICAL GROWTH AND DEVELOPMENT
   Prenatal Life
   The Neonate
   Infancy
   Early Childhood

Exercise C Answer the following questions based on the partial index below.

_____ 1. On what page(s) can information about polar ice caps be found?

_____ 2. Under what entry can information about burned tropical grasslands be found?

_____ 3. Photosynthesis, the process by which plants convert light to energy, can be found under which entry?

_____ 4. Information on the effects of a nuclear explosion might be discussed under which entry?

_____ 5. On which page(s) would information about petroleum be found?

> Fallout 24
> Fire, role in environmental change 17
> Floods 242-247
> Food chains 117
> Forecasting
>   long-term 309
>   retrospective 310
>   short-term 308
> Fossil fuels 487
> Glaciation 78-79

Exercise D Choose one of your textbooks or one from your school library and answer the questions below.

1. Write down the title of the textbook. What does it say about the audience or level? Does it tell you anything else about the book?

_____

_____

_____

_____

2. Who wrote the text? Is the author associated with a school or university? Which one?

_____

3. Turn to the Table of Contents. Is the textbook organized conceptually, chronologically, or a combination of the two?

_____

4. Is there an appendix? If so, describe its contents.

_____

_____

5. Is there a Glossary? _____ Answer Key? _____ Index? _____

Are they listed in the Table of Contents? _____

6. If there is a Glossary, look up the first entry and write it here. _____

Now, see if it is listed in the Index. If so, write the page number(s) where it can be found.

_____

CHAPTER 2

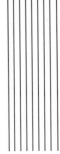

Inside Chapters

Study Objectives

By the end of this chapter, you should be able to:

- locate the basic sections of a chapter;
- interpret various types of illustrations.

Many textbooks have major divisions called **parts**. Each part is further divided into chapters, units, or lessons. Each chapter is organized around one topic or subject. Quickly look through this chapter and decide what the topic is.

_____ parts of a textbook   _____ parts of a chapter

In general, the chapters in a particular textbook are all similarly arranged. This is done so that you can read them more easily. In this chapter, you will learn more about this organization.

2.1 Study Objectives

At the beginning of each chapter in many textbooks is a set of **study objectives**. An objective is something that you try to achieve or reach. Here, the author tells you what you should know or be able to do after reading the chapter. Study objectives always include the most important ideas contained in the reading. Examining them will help you know in advance what points to pay particular attention to.

Look at the study objectives in this chapter. Which objective concerns itself with the section you are studying now?

_____ 1st   _____ 2nd

2.2 Section Titles

Chapters can be divided into **sections**. These sections may be divided into sections called subsections. Sections and subsections may be titled, numbered, or both. Which type is used in this book?

_____ title only _____ number only _____ both

A numbering system might either use a dash (–) or a decimal point (.) between numbers. Look at the section numbers above. Is a dash or a point used?

_____ dash _____ point

The number in front of the dash or point refers to the chapter, and the number after the dash or point refers to the section. For example, the section you are studying now is "section two <u>point</u> two." If a dash were used, it would be read "section two <u>dash</u> two."

2.2

Chapter 2_____↑ ↑____Section 2

2.3 Notes in Margins

Every page in a book has **margins** at the top and the bottom and on the right and left sides. A margin is the empty space between the printed words on a page and the edge of the page. The margins of some textbooks are wide so that authors can write brief notes for you there. These notes refer to information in the text directly beside the notes.

Marginal notes either (1) help you locate key information quickly, or (2) explain something in the passage. Turn to Section 5.1 and count the notes in the margin. Then, read them and decide how many identify information and how many explain information.

total number: _____

number of notes
that identify: _____

number of notes
that explain: _____

2.4 Typographical Clues

Authors often call attention to important words by <u>underlining</u> them, CAPITALIZING them, or by putting them in **boldface** or *italics*. Some textbooks even use different colors to call attention to key words. Words are printed in these ways so that you will notice them immediately. Look through this book to see which of the following are used.

_____ italicizing _____ underlining

_____ boldfacing _____ capitalizing

Important words are printed in special ways the first time the author uses them. After that, they appear in normal print. Turn to the first paragraph in Section 2.3 and answer the following questions.

In which sentence is *margin* printed in boldface?   1 2 3 4 5

In which other sentences does this word occur?   1 2 3 4 5

2.5 Boxed-In Readings

Many textbooks include short, interesting readings which are enclosed in "boxes" having the shape of a rectangle or square. These readings are related in some way to the main reading, but you do not have to read them in order to understand the chapter. Furthermore, the information contained in boxed-in readings seldom appears on examinations. Think of boxed-in readings as extra, optional readings.

A boxed-in reading appears in Chapter 1. In which section is it located, and what topic is it related to?

section number: _____

topic: _____

2.6 Figures and Tables

Illustrations can be divided into two major types. One type, called **tables**, condenses information into a small space so you can read through it quickly and easily. The second type, called **figures**, pictures something to help make the reading clearer. Look quickly through this section and count the number of tables and figures.

total number of tables: _____

total number of figures: _____

You will notice that figures and tables have numbering sytems which are not only independent of each other but also independent of section numbers. For example, in this chapter, there is a Figure 2.1 and also a Table 2.1. Neither one is located in Section 2.1. Find the sections they are found in.

Figure 2.1: _____   Table 2.1: _____

A **table** consists of information which is arranged in rows and columns. At the top of each column there is often a title that identifies its contents. Look at the columns in Table 2.1. What are the titles?

_____   _____

Table 2.1 permits an easy comparison between two types of calendars in use in the world today. Referring to Table 2.1, decide which of the following statements describe the Hegira calendar, which describe the Gregorian calendar, and which are true of both (H = Hegira, G = Gregorian, B = Both).

_____ This calendar has 12 months per year.

_____ This calendar has a greater range of days per month.

_____ This calendar is based upon the moon.

Table 2.1: Gregorian and Hegira Calendars

Gregorian (solar based)		Hegira (lunar based)	
name of month	number of days	name of month	number of days
January	31	Muharram	30
February	28/29	Safar	29
March	31	Rabi I	30
April	30	Rabi II	29
May	31	Jumada I	30
June	30	Jumada II	29
July	31	Rajab	30
August	31	Sha'ban	29
September	30	Ramadan	30
October	31	Shawwal	29
November	30	Dhu'l Qadah	30
December	31	Dhu'l Hejja	29/30

Figures may be of many kinds. An **organization chart** shows the structure of an organization so that you can see the relationship of the various parts to each other. Figure 2.1 illustrates the organization of the United Nations. Look at this figure and answer the following questions.

Which part of the United Nations is the heart of the organization? _____

The United Nations has how many principal parts or organs? _____

The World Health Organization reports to which organ? _____

The High Commissioner for Refugees is administratively linked to which two organs? _____

_____

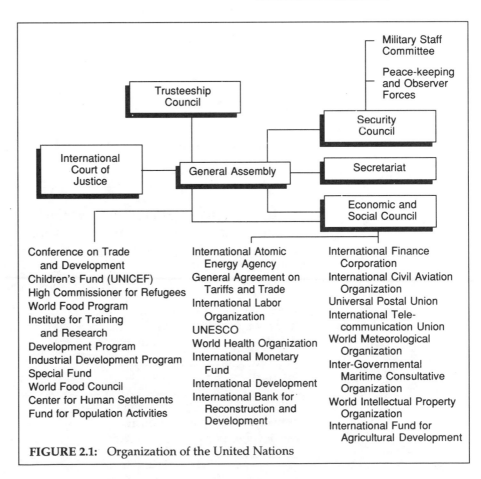

FIGURE 2.1: Organization of the United Nations

A **flow chart** will show you how something is done. Each box in a flow chart represents an action. These boxes are connected by arrows which show the direction of the movement. Figure 2.2 shows how African Sleeping Sickness spreads. Look at this figure and answer the following questions.

What carries the sickness from person to person? _____

Can the sickness be transmitted from people to the tsetse fly? _____

Can people catch this disease directly from infected animals? _____

What is the only way to stop the spread of this disease? _____

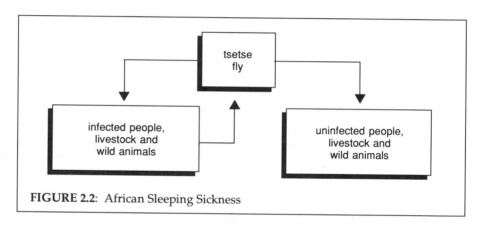

FIGURE 2.2: African Sleeping Sickness

Like a flow chart, a **timeline** shows the order of events. However, a timeline also indicates when these events happened. Figure 2.3 shows significant dates in the history of the computer. Exact dates cannot be determined from this timeline, but you can easily see the order. Look at Figure 2.3 and answer the following questions.

How many people are credited with making contributions toward the development of the computer? _____

In which century after Pascal was little progress made? _____

About how much time passed between Pascal's invention and the development of the first real computer? _____

1600's	Pascal's adding/subtracting device
1700's	
	Leibniz's simple calculator
1800's	Babbage's Difference Machine
	Hollerith's punched cards
	Zuse's simple computer
	Stibitz's remote data processing
1900's	Turing's Colossus I
	First electric digital computer

FIGURE 2.3: Milestones in the Development of the Computer

A **bar graph** shows a comparison of amounts or sizes of things through the use of rectangles (bars). The length of each bar is determined by the quantity or size of the thing being measured. The greater the quantity or size, the longer the bar. Figures 2.4 and 2.5 are examples of bar graphs. Look at them and answer the following questions.

In Figure 2.4, which city is probably farthest from Amsterdam? _____

About how long does it take to fly from Amsterdam to Bonn? _____

In Figure 2.5, which month(s) showed slow sales? _____

About how much money did the ABC Company take in during March and April? _____

Between which two months were the largest gains in sales? _____

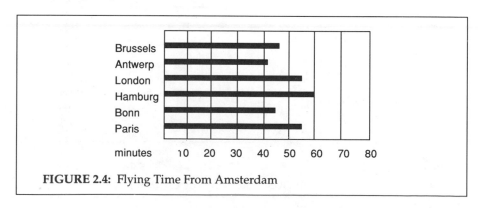

FIGURE 2.4: Flying Time From Amsterdam

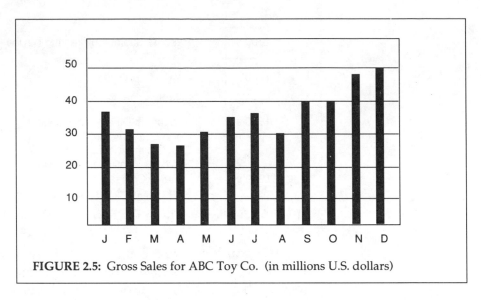

FIGURE 2.5: Gross Sales for ABC Toy Co. (in millions U.S. dollars)

A **line graph** shows the movement of something during a certain period of time. The upward movement of a line represents an increase in something, while the downward movement indicates a decrease. Figure 2.6 is an example of a line graph. Look at this figure and answer the following questions.

In what years did the company suffer declines in profits? _____

In what years did the company show neither growth nor decline in profits? _____

What were ABC's best and worst years? _____

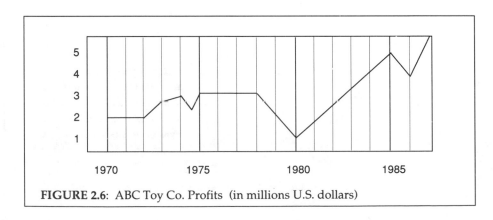

FIGURE 2.6: ABC Toy Co. Profits (in millions U.S. dollars)

A **pie chart** shows the divisions of one whole thing. The circle represents 100% of anything. Each piece of the pie represents a certain percentage of the total. Look at Figure 2.7 and answer the following questions.

What percentage of immigrants came from Europe?

How many years do these statistics cover?

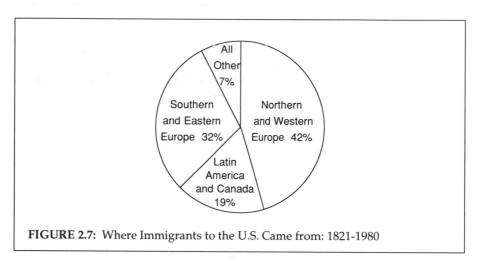

FIGURE 2.7: Where Immigrants to the U.S. Came from: 1821-1980

Drawings and photographs are occasionally used in textbooks to illustrate things being talked about in a chapter. Figure 2.8 shows drawings from a psychology book. Examine them and explain what concept they illustrate.

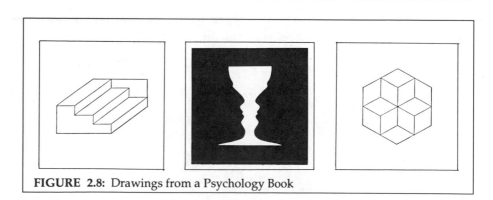

FIGURE 2.8: Drawings from a Psychology Book

2.7 Chapter Summaries

The last part of a chapter often contains a brief review of the key points in the chapter. This is called a **summary**. Compare this chapter's summary with the study objectives. Which one is more detailed?

_____ summary   _____ study objectives

2.8 Vocabulary Lists

Some textbooks contains vocabulary lists. A **vocabulary list** includes key terms and expressions that are introduced in a chapter. This list is usually located at the end of each chapter. Definitions of these words can be found in the chapter or in the glossary (see Section 1.6). Find the vocabulary list in this chapter and answer the following questions.

What is it called? _____

How are words listed?   _____ alphabetically

_____ in the order they are
presented in the textbook

2.9 Reading Lists

Many textbooks also include reading lists. In the reading list, the author recommends books that can provide additional information about the ideas included in the chapter. Reading lists are found at the end of each chapter. Go to the reading list in this chapter. What is the name of this section? How many books are listed?

name of section: _____

number of books: _____

The last entry from this chapter's reading list is reprinted below. Each part of the entry is identified for you.

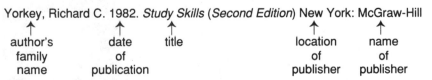

2.10 Review Questions

This section consists of questions or problems for you to answer. These exercises serve two purposes: (1) to check your understanding of the material; and (2) to provide opportunities to apply the information or skills you learned in the chapter. The review questions in this book are divided into two types. What are their names?

type 1: _____

type 2: _____

Summary

In this chapter, you examined the parts of a typical chapter. You saw that the author may use a number of ways to emphasize important ideas. These can be discovered by examining the following:

1. study objectives
2. section titles
3. notes in margins
4. special typography
5. chapter summaries
6. vocabulary lists

The value and purpose of illustrations were also discussed. You learned that textbooks generally divide illustrations into tables and figures, the latter group comprising many types of illustrations.

Key Vocabulary

bar graph	italicizing	study objectives
boldfacing	line graph	summary
boxed-in readings	notes in margin	table
chapter	organization chart	timeline
figure	review questions	vocabulary list
flow chart		

Recommended Reading

Bradley, Anne. 1983. *Take Note of College Study Skills*. Glenview, IL: Scott, Foresman. See Chapter 8 on illustrations.

Dubin, Fraida and Elite Olshtain. 1981. *Reading by All Means*. Reading, MA: Addison-Wesley. See Chapters 3 and 4 on textbook organization.

Eisenberg, Anne. 1978. *Reading Technical Books*. Englewood Cliffs, NJ: Prentice-Hall. See Chapters 8-10 on textbook organization.

Hamp-Lyons, Liz and Karen Berry Courter. 1984. *Research Matters*. Rowley, MA: Newbury House. See Chapter 2 on basic library skills.

Rosenthal, Lisa and Susan Blake Rowland. 1986. *Academic Reading and Study Skills for International Students*. Englewood Cliffs, N.J: Prentice Hall. See Part 3 of Chapter 4 and Part 2 of Chapter 7 on illustrations.

Yorkey, Richard C. 1982. *Study Skills (Second Edition)*. New York: McGraw-Hill. See the section on textbook reading in Chapter 6.

Thought Questions

1. As you now know, textbooks are similar to other types of books, but in certain ways they are different. Compare a textbook with a novel by completing the following table.

Textbooks Vs. Novels

Components of Books	Textbook	Novel
Title Page	*yes*	*yes*
Table of Contents		
Appendix		
Glossary		
Index		
Chapters		
Vocabulary Lists		
Study Objectives		
Notes in Margins		

2. What kinds of information can be found in the left margin of a textbook page? bottom margin? top margin?

3. How are study objectives similar to chapter summaries? How do they differ?

4. In what two other locations in this textbook can you find the terms in the Key Vocabulary lists?

5. Which kinds of textbooks would you expect to find drawings in? Which would you expect to find photographs in?

Exercises

Exercise A Find the key terms in each passage and underline them.

1. Buying low and selling high is one sure way to make a profit. Arbitrage is the process of buying at a lower price in one market and selling higher in another.

2. When a force acts on a body, it can deform the body, change its state of motion, or both. Forces can be classified into either contact forces or action-at-a-distance forces. An example of the latter is gravity.

3. Learning a language parallels the more general process of learning a culture. Acculturation is a lifelong process in which imitation, verbal instruction, and inference all play a part.

4. An ecosystem refers to the community of living things, together with its physical environment existing in some part of nature.

5. A formula that gives the relative number of atoms of each element present in a formula

unit is called an empirical formula because it is normally derived from the results of some experimental analysis.

6. The production process for a television commercial may be divided into three stages. First is the phase in which detailed production plans are developed: the preproduction phase. Second is the actual production of the various elements of the commercial: the production phase. Finally is the process in which the various elements of the commercial are combined into a finished product: the finishing phase.

7. Long before cities came about, the common needs of people were satisfied through the establishment of communities. A community is a concentration of people whose primary economic and social needs can be met within the immediate area.

8. Before any kind of research can be conducted, investigators must be able to define the population under study. A population is a systemi-cally defined group of anything. The things that constitute this group, the members, may range from Urdu speakers to kinds of computers.

9. Deduction reasons from the general to the particular. Because it is extensively used in syllogisms, it is sometimes known as syllogistic reasoning. The first statement of a simple syllogism is called a major premise. It defines a group of objects having shared characteristics. The second statement of a simple syllogism is called a minor premise. It defines another group and identifies them as belonging to the first group. The third statement is called a conclusion. It is a logical result of the two premises.

10. Four blood types exist: A, B, AB, and O. This classification system is based on the presence or absence of substances called agglutinatives which cause a thickening of red blood cells when mixed with alien blood that does not contain them.

Exercise B Using a textbook other than this one, answer the following questions.

1. What is the title of the textbook and who is the author?

   _____

2. Open the book to the beginning of any chapter and write the chapter title.

   _____

3. Does this chapter include study objectives? If so, write the first one here.

   _____

   _____

4. Read the titles of the chapter sections. Does your book number the sections? _____ If so, are dashes or decimal points used?

   _____

5. Based only upon the chapter title and the section titles, write a sentence that summarizes the main ideas of the chapter.

   _____

   _____

6. Read the opening paragraph of the chapter. Does it summarize the contents of the chapter? _____

7. Does your chapter contain a summary? Read it and compare its contents with your answer to the preceding question.

8. Does your chapter have a vocabulary list? If so, write the first entry here: _____.
   Turn to the back of your book and see if there is a glossary. If so, and if your word is listed,

write the definition below. If there is no glossary, or if your word is not listed in the glossary, check the index and find the definition in the reading.

_____

_____

9. Is there a list of suggested readings in your chapter? _____

10. Does your text have review questions? What are they called?

_____

11. If the chapter contains other sections, list the names of these sections here.

_____

_____

_____

_____

CHAPTER 3

Conceptual Development

Study Objectives

By the end of this chapter, you should be able to:

- identify how authors organize and present ideas in textbooks.

A great deal of thought goes into the effective organization of ideas or concepts. When deciding how to arrange their ideas effectively, authors can choose from a large number of approaches. A single approach may continue for many pages, or it may last only a few sentences.

Studies indicate that an awareness of the organization of passages will help you in understanding and remembering what you read (Carrell 1985). In this chapter, you will study a few of the most common types of conceptual organization found in textbooks.

3.1 First to Last

In this approach, the author arranges events according to their order in time. The most common form, **chronological order**, arranges events from the most distant to the most recent. **Reverse chronological order** arranges events in the opposite way. Consider the following passages from physics, medical science, and history.

> In the distant past, scientists viewed the earth as the center of the universe. One of the earliest documented models of this view was that of Claudius Ptolemy, a Greek astronomer who lived in the second century. This view went unchallenged for the next 1,400

years until a Polish astronomer, Nicolaus Copernicus, proposed that the earth as well as the other planets orbited the sun. The work of Danish astronomer Tycho Brahe, who was born three years after Copernicus died, provided the basis for the model of the solar system which is accepted today.

Which way is this passage arranged?

_____ chronological order

_____ reverse chronological order

List the names of the scientists in the order they are presented.

Ptolemy, _____, and then

_____

In the fight against malaria, scientists are studying ways to develop an effective vaccine. This tactic is quite different from those used over thirty years ago. At that time, the World Health Organization led a major effort to eradicate this disease, and a number of methods were employed to kill the disease-carrying mosquito. Prominent among them was the use of DDT, which did indeed kill mosquitos, but also brought harm to the environment.

Which way is this passage arranged?

_____ chronological order

_____ reverse chronological order

In the order they are mentioned, list the weapons used in the war against malaria.

_____ and _____

Writing is thought to have originated in the Middle East with the Sumerians about 3100 B.C. Its earliest use was in keeping business records, but over the years laws and medical records were also written down. When writing was taught in schools, it became available to many people. In due course, writers began recording history and later developed extensive tracts on philosophy, science, and literature.

Which way is this passage arranged?

_____ chronological order

_____ reverse chronological order

In the passage above, the author uses various words to show time. Locate and underline them.

A **process** is another way of arranging events in the order they occur. A process consists of steps which are arranged from beginning to end. Each step in a process represents a single action.

> One way to separate mixtures into their components is through distillation. For example, assume a solution of sodium chloride. The first step in this process is to boil the solution in a flask. The steam is then converted into water by passing it through a condenser. The water, now separated from the salt, is collected in a container.

This process is **linear** in form, meaning that the steps or historical events occur in a straight line and have a beginning and an end. Another type of process is **cyclical**. This means that the steps move continuously in a circle. A description of a cyclical process can begin with any step.

Examine the following passages, taken from biology and ecology, and fill in the diagrams that follow them.

> When animals respire, oxygen is breathed in and carbon dioxide is breathed out. This carbon dioxide is then taken in by plants, which release oxygen.

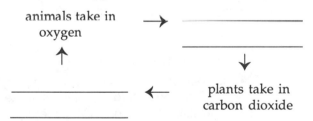

> For many years, consumers in the United States have preferred to purchase canned instead of bottled beverages. Unlike glass bottles, aluminum cans were simply thrown away after their contents were drunk. In the early 1970s, however, efforts began to reclaim and recycle these cans in order to conserve aluminum supplies. After use, cans are collected and crushed into bales. They are subsequently sent off to factories where they are melted and rolled into sheets. These sheets are then used in the manufacture of more cans, which in turn are used in the packaging of beverages. These beverages are sold to consumers, and the process begins anew.

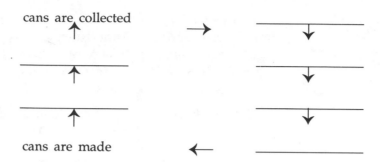

cans are collected

cans are made

3.2 Least to Most Important

In this approach, authors present the least important points first and save the most important points for last. Consider these examples, the first taken from business and the second from history.

In any large business enterprise, three levels of management can be identified. The lowest level, operating management, is charged with the day-to-day supervision of workers. The next division, middle management, is made up of general managers and plant superintendents. They are responsible for implementing broad plans. The highest level, top management, develops policies.

least important level: _____

↓   _____

most important level: _____

A number of names are associated with classical physics, which was developed before the nineteenth century. Galileo Galilei studied the laws of motion in the presence of constant acceleration. Johannes Kepler developed laws to explain the motion of the planets. James Maxwell advanced a unified theory of electromagnetism. But the most important contributions were provided by Isaac Newton, who developed classical physics as a systematic theory.

classical physicists
of lesser importance: _____

_____

_____

_____

most important
classical physicist: _____

3.3 Known to Unknown

Authors will sometimes first present familiar information and then move on to new, unfamiliar information. The following example, taken from chemistry, illustrates this approach.

> Nearly everyone knows the important role oxygen plays in our lives. Without it, we could not survive. Fortunately, oxygen can be found everywhere and in abundant supplies. The atmosphere is nearly 20% oxygen. Oxygen is also a constituent of water, forming 89% of its mass. This element also has the distinction of being the most abundant element in the earth's crust—nearly 94% when measured by volume.

probably known
to reader: We need oxygen to live.

probably unknown
to reader: Atmosphere is _____% oxygen.
_____ is 89% oxygen.

Oxygen forms _____% of the earth's crust.

Another way of moving to the unknown from the known is through an analogy. An analogy uncovers similarities in two things that otherwise are quite different. Look at the following example.

> Just as water flows from high ground to low ground, so air flows from high pressure to low pressure.

water is compared to _____

ground is compared to _____

You are quite likely to be familiar with the principle involved with the movement of water. The example takes advantage of this knowledge to show how the movement of water is similar to the movement of air. In this case, the analogy was quite brief. A more complicated concept may make use of a longer analogy. Suppose, for instance, that the author of an astronomy text is trying to explain how the universe changes over time. An analogy might clarify the problem:

> When walking though a forest, we will observe trees at various stages of development. Some are young, some are old, some are dead. On the ground we might spot seeds. Although our visit to the forest is brief and we cannot witness the entire life cycle of a

tree, we have enough evidence around us to guess how a tree develops. So it is with stars in the universe.

forest is compared to _____

_____ is compared to our lifetime

_____ is compared to stars and planets

Although an analogy can be useful, it has limitations because no two things are exactly alike. Look at the following example.

Both the earth and an onion are made up of layers, but the similarity between the two ends there. Each layer of an onion is composed of the same substance and has the same thickness, while the earth's layers vary.

earth is compared to _____

points of similarity: _____

points of difference: _____

3.4 Cause and Effect

In this approach, the author argues that one action makes another one happen. Consider the prospect of a nuclear war. Some scientists believe that environmental damage from a nuclear war will not be limited to the area where the explosions occur. They believe that huge clouds of dust will form in the atmosphere, covering much of the earth and blocking out needed sunlight for quite a long time. The absence of sunlight will lower temperatures. These actions are known as a "nuclear winter."

cause = _____

possible effect = _____

Sometimes, the opposite approach is used. That is, the author identifies an event and then tries to explain what made it happen. An example of this can be seen in the following passage from child psychology.

It has long been observed that in the first few months of life, infants show no preference for using the right or the left hand. By the time they reach adulthood, however, nearly 95% of all people will be right-handed, with the remaining 5% being either left-handed or ambidextrous. In determining the reason for this, many researchers have focused on the role that environment and genetic direction may play.

known effect   =   _____

_____ = environment, heredity

An event may happen because of something else that happened shortly before it (the immediate cause) or long before it (the remote cause). An example from history illustrates this.

Historians find it useful to distinguish between distant and immediate causes for the outbreak of the First World War. Long-simmering causes include various factors which heightened international tension before 1914: the rise of nationalism, disputes over territories, economic competition, imperialist policies of some countries, and the absence of an effective international organization to air grievances and keep the peace. The event which marked the outbreak of hostilities was the assassination of Archduke Francis Ferdinand of Austria in 1914.

Which word is used to indicate that the causes are

remote? _____

The effects of any particular action or event may last a short or long time. Consider the following example, taken from psychology.

When people are exposed to high levels of noise at unpredictable intervals, the effects are both immediate and noticeable. One physiological change is a rapid increase in the heart rate. Behaviorally, these people tend to make a greater number of errors in whatever activity they are engaged in. Prolonged exposure to noise promotes what has been called a "filtering mechanism." In other words, people simply cease paying attention to the noise. They then cease making excessive numbers of errors.

cause: *high level of noise*_____

short-term effects: _____

_____

long-term effects: _____

_____

The effects of any given action may be expected or unexpected, desirable or undesirable. To illustrate this, let us examine a problem taken from civil engineering.

In order to curtail speeding, zigzags (a special road design that forces vehicles to make sharp turns in alternating directions) were installed in front of every intersection. As it turned out, vehicles did indeed slow down. They had to in order to pass through the zigzagged path. This was both desirable and expected. However, a driver wishing to turn at intersections where there were zigzags could not signal an intention to do so because the sharp alternating turns of the vehicle shut off the turning signal. This effect was clearly unexpected and undesirable.

cause: _____

positive effect: _____

negative effect: _____

The effect of one action sometimes becomes the cause for another action. Actions which are all causally related form a causal chain. The "links" in this chain can continue indefinitely. An example of this is taken from ecology.

The widespread use of a manmade family of chemicals called chlorofluorocarbons is thought to be causing the deterioration of the ozone layer, which helps to filter out harmful rays from the sun. This deterioration is helping to raise the temperature of the earth's surface, producing what has been called a "greenhouse effect." A continuing increase of this problem might cause a melting of the polar ice caps. The ensuing flooding would present a danger to coastal cities.

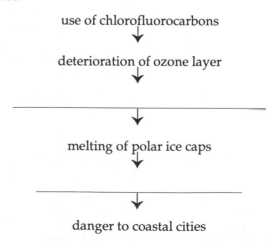

A causal relationship does not automatically exist simply because one event happens after another one. Consider the following:

> An increase in the crime rate roughly coincided with an economic depression.

It may be, of course, that the health of an economy does indeed influence criminal activity. You might even think that it is reasonable to assume such a causal relationship. However, it may be that other factors are responsible for a higher rate of crime. Careful authors take great pains to ensure that the proper cause is attributed to a particular effect. Consider the following example, taken from social science.

> A number of studies have been conducted which aimed to examine a possible relationship between population density and crime. Research has clearly established that city neighborhoods with the highest density also have the highest crime rates. One might therefore conclude that crowding causes crime. However, it has been noted that these same neighborhoods are also the poorest neighborhoods. It is quite possible that poverty is in fact the cause of both the high density and the high crime rates.

_____ : *crime* _____

apparent cause: _____

possible cause: _____

3.5 General and Specific Instances

In this approach, the author makes a broad statement which may range from an unproven proposition or hypothesis to a self-evident and accepted principle, law, or axiom. These statements are then followed by examples which serve one of two purposes: (1) to illustrate the statement so the reader can understand it better; or (2) to prove the validity of the statement.

> Liquidity refers to how easily an asset can be turned into cash. A house is an example of a relatively illiquid asset. On the other hand, a savings account tends to be very liquid.

general: *liquidity* _____

specific: _____

_____

Fires resulting from an earthquake are responsible for more damage than the earthquake itself. The earthquake of 1906 in San Francisco ruptured many gas lines, starting the fires that destroyed most of the city.

general: _____

specific: _____

In the discussion of liquidity, examples are given in order to show you which assets are considered to be illiquid and which are liquid. Examples are used here merely to illustrate the concept. The discussion of earthquakes, however, makes use of an example in order to prove the claim that earthquake-related fires are highly destructive forces. The author's claim becomes believable because an example supports it. Decide in the following two passages why examples are used.

There can be no doubt that externally caused frustration often leads to aggression. Many studies have documented that children whose toys are out of reach may scream until someone gives them one.

_____ illustrate _____ prove

A number of substances are added to oil to permit it to be used at higher temperatures. These include compounds of barium, calcium, zinc, and chlorine.

_____ illustrate _____ prove

A passage might be arranged from **specific to general** as well. Here, the author begins by offering an example, a fact or a particular instance. This is followed by a statement, idea, or principle having a general application. A psychology reading might cite a particular type of human behavior and then formulate a hypothesis to explain why people behave in this way. An economics reading might present a study of the fiscal policies in Country X, and then propose a theory to explain them. Examine the following passage from biology.

It has long been observed that deer generally spend their lives inside an area of 2 square miles, that rabbits live within a 14-acre area, and that mice occupy only a small part of one acre. Although these and other animals will temporarily leave their established territories for food, they usually will return quickly.

specific: _____

general: _____

3.6 Problem and Solution

With this type of development, the author first asks a question or presents a problem and then provides an answer or proposes a solution.

If a tree falls in the woods and no one is there to hear it, will there be a sound? Some people will say "no" and insist that sound is a sensory experience which requires a listener to perceive it. Others will say "yes" and point out that sound is simply a movement of molecules caused by a vibrating body. We will avoid this age-old debate by suggesting that both answers are partially right. Hearing requires vibrations as well as the reception of those vibrations by the ear.

problem: _____

solution: _____

At present rates of consumption, world supplies of oil and natural gas are expected to last only another fifty years or so. Much attention has therefore been focused on the development of other energy sources. Of these, coal, synthetic fuels, and nuclear power will probably play the largest roles, but solar and wind power will no doubt contribute in significant ways as well in easing this problem.

problem: _____

solution: _____

3.7 Whole to Parts

In this type of development, the author identifies an entity or system and then separates it into its parts. Sometimes, the reverse approach is presented. The two passages which follow illustrate this. Fill in the blanks for each one.

The atmosphere of the earth today contains approximately 78 percent nitrogen, 21 percent oxygen, and 1 percent of trace gases including argon, carbon dioxide, neon, and helium.

whole: _____

parts: _____ (78%)

_____ (21%)

_____ (1%)

Matter, under certain circumstances and in certain combinations, forms minerals. Likewise, minerals form rocks. Rocks form the outer layer of the earth, which is called the crust.

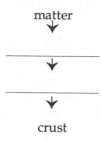

matter

crust

When a whole has a great number of parts, it is useful to group these parts according to shared characteristics. This system of grouping is called **classification**. Each element of this whole will be placed in a particular category or class. There are, of course, endless ways of classifying the various elements of a whole, and how an author chooses to do this depends upon the purpose. In the exercise below, how might the professionals listed on the left want to classify people?

_____ 1. biologist   a. by income

_____ 2. psychologist   b. by language

_____ 3. linguist   c. by age or race

_____ 4. economist   d. by mental health

Categories in classification systems frequently have subdivisions. For example, a sociologist who groups people according to nationality might wish to have a more precise idea of a person's location. The following subdivisions would help:

country
↓
state/province
↓
county
↓
town/city
↓
street

The following passage contains an example of classification from business. Read the passage and complete the diagram.

Because the products in industrialized countries are numerous, it is helpful to group them. One system of classification is based upon how long these products last. Durables have an economic life of three or more years. Examples include automobiles, furniture, and major appliances. Semidurables last from six months to three years. Clothing and canned or frozen foods are semidurable products. Nondurables, such as fresh foods, last only up to six months.

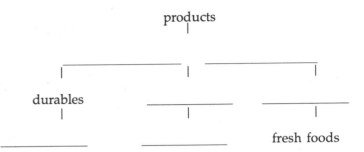

3.8 Concept to Description

In this approach, the author identifies and sometimes defines the concept to be introduced and then discusses its characteristics, applications, purpose, or value. Occasionally, the author groups characteristics into positive and negative traits. Look at the three passages below, the first taken from meteorology, the second from computer science, and the third from business.

A tornado is a circle of rapidly moving air. It is most visible to us when condensation occurs or when debris is picked up from the earth's surface and travels through the spiraling funnel. The funnel looks as though it is attached to the base of a cloud. It often touches the ground for a short time and then rises again. Great destruction can occur when it does touch the ground.

concept: _____

A computer is a system of electromechanical devices that receives data, processes this data arithmetically or logically, and then makes this information available to the user. Like all technological innovations, computers have their advantages and disadvantages. They are extremely fast and accurate, can store huge amounts of information, and enable us to compute complex statistical data that we otherwise would not be able to. On the other hand, computers can be expensive to purchase and operate. They need very precise instructions, and they have a limited ability to generalize and use inductive reasoning.

concept: _____

positive
traits: _____ __

_____

negative
traits: _____

_____

An agreement between two or more parties who voluntarily agree to act or not to act in a particular way is called a contract. All valid contracts contain common features. First, there must be an offer by one party and an acceptance by another. Second, the parties entering the contract must do so willingly. In addition, the parties to the contract must be legally sane and of legal age. Next, the parties must exchange something of value such as money, property or a promise to do work. Finally, whatever is exchanged must be legal.

concept: _____

number of traits: _____

3.9 Similarities and Differences

In this approach, authors compare two or more things by identifying ways in which these things are similar and different. One way of doing this is to place points of comparison next to each other so you can easily see how they are alike and how they differ. Look at the following passage, taken from medicine, to see how this can be done. Then complete the chart.

The common cold is called just that because nearly everyone has come down with it many times. Influenza ("flu" for short) is less common and far more serious. Both sicknesses are characterized by coughing, blocked-up nasal passages, sore throats, and sneezing. Distinguishing symptoms include low fever and minor aching for colds, but high fever and much aching for flus.

SYMPTOMS	COLDS	INFLUENZA
coughing	*yes*	*yes*
aching		
blocked-up noses		
sore throats		
fever		
sneezing		

Another approach to comparison is to discuss one thing in its entirety and then discuss the second thing. When authors use this approach, the work of comparing is placed on you. Consider the following passage, taken from business. Use it to complete the chart.

> The oldest, simplest, and most common form of business is the sole proprietorship. This is a business owned and operated by one person. The owner has a right to all profits and can exercise complete authority over operations. However, sole proprietorships are quite limited in size and finances.

> At the other extreme is the corporation. A corporation is a business usually having a great number of owners. Profits sometimes are divided among these owners, sometimes are reinvested in the business, and sometimes are split between both. Authority is diluted among many managers who are responsible to a board of directors. A corporation's size and finances have no limit.

CHARACTERISTICS	SOLE PROPRIETORSHIPS	CORPORATIONS
number of owners		
profits		
authority		
size		
finances		

Quite frequently, comparisons are indirectly stated in order to economize on words. In the following passage, computers and humans are compared with respect to information processing skills. Although very little is mentioned about humans, you can easily see the differences and similarities.

In information processing, computers will outperform humans in almost every category. Computers operate at extremely high speeds without tiring. They process information without making mistakes. Their memories are virtually unlimited. Only in one area do computers score less than humans: Computers require specific instructions in order to complete tasks.

Describe the information processing capabilities of humans by circling the appropriate answers:

operate at high speeds	operate at low speeds
become tired	work tirelessly
make mistakes	are accurate
limited memory	unlimited memory
precise instructions needed	can perform tasks without instructions

Summary

In this chapter, you studied ways that authors commonly organize and develop their ideas. Concepts are frequently presented according to their appearance in time, their degree of importance, their level of difficulty, their causal relationship, the relationship of components to a whole, and the ways in which they are similar and different. You saw that by recognizing typical patterns of development, you can predict the direction the author is taking.

Key Vocabulary

analogy	chronological order	classification	process

Recommended Reading

Sonka, Amy. 1981. *Skillful Reading.* Englewood Cliffs, NJ: Prentice-Hall. See Chapter 4 on classification, Chapter 5 on contrast, Chapter 6 on chronological order, Chapter 7 on process, and Chapter 8 on cause/effect.

Thought Questions

1. In the preface of this book, a textbook is compared to a beast. In what ways is this analogy accurate? How does a textbook differ from a beast?

2. Name one process from each of the following disciplines: chemistry, physics, biology, economics, and archaeology.

3. When you think of chronological order, a history textbook might come to mind. What other kinds of textbooks might be arranged chronologically? Conceptually?

4. Superstitions come about because of faulty reasoning in determining the proper cause for a particular effect. For example, it is said that if a person's nose itches, money will soon come to that person. If there is no necessary relationship between cause and effect here, how do you suppose this superstition came to be? Think of another superstition and speculate as to its origin.

5. How is the management of an organization like the skeleton of a body? How is the splash made by a stone thrown into a pool of water like the introduction of a new product to the market?

Exercises

Exercise A The following passages contain analogies. Find the corresponding items and write them in the blanks below.

1. A camera uses lenses to bring rays of light into focus. In like manner, an electron microscope uses electromagnets to focus beams of electrons.

   a. _____ = electron microscope

   b. _____ = electromagnets

   c. _____ = beams of electrons

2. A person's head is something like a walnut. The walnut has a hard outer shell that protects the meat inside.

   a. _____ = walnut

   b. _____ = outer shell

   c. _____ = meat

3. Psychology can be thought of as the hub of a wheel. Each spoke represents another field or profession.

   a. _____ = all fields of study

   b. _____ = psychology

   c. _____ = each field

4. The apparent movement of stars in our galaxy is analogous to the traffic movement on a busy highway. All the cars around us are going in the same direction and at approximately the same speed, but some are changing lanes and others are passing each other.

   a. cars = _____

   b. highway = _____

5. When studying chemistry, it is important to learn the chemical symbols before learning formulas. This is a bit like learning to spell. We learn the letters of the alphabet in order to form words.

   a. _____ = _____

   b. _____ = _____

6. The different galaxies in the universe seem to be held together by the gravitational attraction of everything contained in the galaxy. The sizes of the galaxies themselves probably do not change, but the distances between galaxies are probably increasing. This notion might make better sense if we picture a balloon which is covered with dots. As the balloon is inflated, each dot moves away from its neighbors.

a. _____ = _____

b. _____ = _____

7. Plate tectonics is a theory explaining the shape of the earth's surface. The top layer of the earth, the lithosphere, is broken in several places. To visualize this, picture an orange. If we peel the orange and then replace each piece, we would have a situation quite close to the plates on the earth.

a. _____ = _____

b. _____ = _____

8. When you use a telephone, your call first passes through a central exchange before another phone rings. It is this exchange that makes the connection. The nervous system of the body operates in a similar manner. Various nerves connect the central nervous system with the rest of the body. When a signal is sent from one part of the body to another, it passes through the brain or the spinal cord.

a. _____ = _____

b. _____ = _____

9. A battery must be kept charged, but not overcharged. The voltage regulator controls the amount of electricity which goes to the battery. Living organisms also have regulating agents in the form of enzymes. Enzymes are molecules of protein which control the flow of energy throughout the body. Enzymes help the organism function in a stable fashion.

a. _____ = _____

b. _____ = _____

Exercise B In the space next to each passage below, write the letter of the type of conceptual development used.

a. simple cause-effect
b. causal chain
c. chronological order
d. analogy
e. classification
f. linear process
g. cyclical process
h. problem to solution
i. description
j. comparison

_____ **1.** Both bacteria and viruses are extremely small. Bacteria differ from viruses in that they are cellular. They contain both RNA and DNA, whereas viruses contain one or the other but never both. Bacteria are also able to reproduce themselves, but viruses cannot.

_____ **2.** Mexico City is located in a basin about 7,500 feet above sea level. The city is surrounded by mountains from which many small rivers flow to form a series of shallow lakes.

_____ **3.** When manufactured products are used, they all too frequently are simply discarded. This is hardly an efficient way to conserve limited resources. One way of dealing with this dilemma is through the practice of recycling, whereby these products are collected and used again. Recycling not only helps us to avoid needless waste of resources, but it also improves the appearance of the environment.

_____ 4. Consumers can become brand loyal simply by picking one brand, trying it and then evaluating it. If the performance of the brand is satisfactory to them, they may stop their search and consistently purchase the same brand. Should the brand prove unsatisfactory, they buy another brand. This continues until they become happy with one brand.

_____ 5. The nuclear age was born on August 6, 1945, when the first atomic bomb was exploded over Hiroshima, Japan. Seven years later, The United States tested the first hydrogen bomb over the Bikini Atoll in the Pacific Ocean. Soon, the Soviet Union developed its own atomic and hydrogen bombs. Since then, the number of countries in possession of the bomb has grown.

_____ 6. When a country is invaded by a foreign army, the invaded country fights to protect itself as best it can. In effect, this is what happens when foreign particles enter your body. White blood cells, acting as a line of defense, attack and try to neutralize these particles.

_____ 7. Headaches involve a disturbance of blood flow in the brain. When blood vessels expand or shrink, they stimulate highly sensitive nerve endings

found in the blood vessels themselves. This is what is responsible for the pain experienced — not the nerve endings in the brain itself because they are insensitive to pain.

_____ 8. When water at the surface of the ocean is warmed, it evaporates. As the vapor rises, it is cooled by the wind and forms droplets of liquid water. These droplets accumulate to form clouds which are carried toward land by winds. At some point, precipitation occurs as rain or snow. Much of this precipitation enters creeks, streams, and rivers which ultimately carry the water back to the ocean.

_____ 9. Any discussion of biochemistry must address the major types of biomolecules and their functions. Nearly all of them can be grouped into one of four categories: proteins, carbohydrates, lipids, and nucleic acids.

_____ 10. Lakes require nutrients to sustain the life of the organisms living in them. However, too much nourishment can be undesirable because it increases the growth of algae. The algae deplete the oxygen supply, killing fish and other marine life. These dead organisms further contaminate the lake, eventually killing almost all life except certain bacteria.

Exercise C The concepts in the following two readings are developed through the use of a combination of approaches. Read the passages carefully and answer the questions that follow them.

Societies

In a biological sense, a society is any community of organisms characterized by an extensive division of labor and internal organization. Humans, of course, form societies, but so do other forms of life. In addition to certain species of mammals are insects such as termites, ants, bees, and wasps. Insect and human societies are similar in some aspects, but quite different in others.

Activity in insect societies revolves around the queen. In bee colonies, her family consists of workers, drones, and sometimes soldiers. Workers sometimes serve as nurses for the first few weeks of their life. They then assume other duties in the colony such as cleaning house or guarding the entrances. Finally, they may become field bees, seeking out food. Drones are male bees that have no sting and do no work. Their function is to mate with the queen for reproductive purposes. Individual bees have no choice in their roles. All of this is determined for them.

A human society usually consists of many individuals and families. The division of labor is not biologically determined, and changes in behavior can be brought about by learning. Both types of societies function effectively and both are biologically successful.

1. Complete the following classification scheme.

Societies
|

| |
| |

———————— other life forms
| |

———————
| | | |

bees ——— ——— ———
|

| | | |

———— ———— ———— ————

2. The following table compares human and bee societies. Complete it by putting checkmarks in the appropriate columns.

CHARACTERISTICS	HUMAN SOCIETIES	BEE SOCIETIES
One individual is the focus of all activity.		
Some members of society change jobs/duties throughout their lives.		
Members of society have some choice as to what these jobs duties are.		
This type of society functions effectively from a biological point of view.		

3. Although all insect societies are quite similar in their division of labor and internal organization, human societies differ from each other. Describe the division of labor in your society, and compare it with another society if possible.

_____

_____

_____

_____

_____

_____

_____

_____

Schistosomiasis

Perhaps the most feared disease in the world today is one with a tongue-twisting name: **schistosomiasis**. Affecting both people and animals in rural areas, "schisto" results from a lack of proper sanitary safeguards. In this regard, it is a particularly tragic disease because it is avoidable.

Schistosomiasis is caused by a parasite called the **schistosome**. The life cycle of the schistosome begins when its larvae leave snails found in water. These larvae then penetrate the skin of animals or humans where they grow into worms. The worms then lay eggs, some of which find their way to other parts of the body while others leave the body through wastes. If the eggs reach water, they again hatch into larvae and seek out snails. Thus, the cycle is repeated.

In humans, the effects of the disease may not be noticed for years. When symptoms do eventually surface, they are frequently in the form of extreme exhaustion owing to irreversible damage to the heart, lungs, kidneys, and liver. Those afflicted with the disease die an early death.

Attempts to control schisto have been largely unsuccessful. The schistosome cycle is able to continue uninterrupted because in rural areas it is common practice to use the same water sources for everything from washing to waste disposal. Those who already have contracted the disease can seek treatment, but it is expensive and often requires hospitalization. The use of chemicals to kill the snails would harm other marine life. Given the difficulty of breaking the life cycle and the unlikelihood that people will change their ways, the best hope lies in the development of a vaccine. This will take many years, and it is unfortunate but inevitable that the number of people falling victim to schistosomiasis will increase before a solution is found.

1. Draw a flow chart of the life cycle of the schistosome.

2. Explain ways in which the cycle can be broken.

3. A symptom of schisto is extreme tiredness. Show how a different cause (illness) might be attributed to this effect (symptom).

4. Speculate as to why the victims of schisto are largely from rural areas.

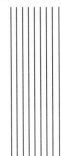

Helps and Hindrances in Reading

Study Objectives

By the end of this chapter, you should be able to:

- understand the significance of words called markers which help show the form of a reading;
- use these markers to predict meaning;
- analyze structures that are responsible for making certain sentences or paragraphs difficult to read and understand.

Readings contain small but important markers that help you to follow the structure or form of a reading. Among others, Nuttall (1982) claims that by paying attention to these words and knowing how they operate, you can use them to make the reading easier to understand. You can see the useful role these markers play by comparing the following two paragraphs.

> Chromium is a hard and shiny metal which resists corrosion. Chromium does not deteriorate at a rapid rate. Industrial use of this element is quite common. The door handles of many automobiles are coated with chromium.

> Chromium is a hard and shiny metal which resists corrosion. In other words, chromium does not deteriorate at a rapid rate. For this reason, industrial use of this element is quite common. For example, the door handles of many automobiles are coated with chromium.

Although these two paragraphs contain the same information, the first one is more difficult to follow because no markers are used. In the next few sections, you will learn more about the use of these markers.

Following that, you will learn about certain types of sentences that cause difficulty with reading.

4.1 Sequencing and Enumeration Markers

As you saw in Section 3.1, events are usually arranged in the order that they occur. These events may be stages in a process or simply things that happen in chronological order. Certain words called sequencing markers (see Table 4.1) can be used to show you when one event ends and another begins. Observe how **sequencing markers** are used in the following passage.

> The Industrial Revolution in Europe came about in several steps. The first machines in the eighteenth century made use of naturally existing power sources, such as moving water, to drive weaving machines. These were soon replaced, however, by the steam-driven engine. At roughly the same time, it was discovered that coke could be extracted from coal. Coke became a new fuel, used primarily to make steel. Eventually, an extensive transportation and communications network developed in order for industries to better serve their markets.

Which word marks the beginning action? _____

Which markers show the next two actions?

_____   _____

Which marker shows the last action?   _____

TABLE 4.1: Sequencing Markers

Beginning Action	first, to begin/start with in the first step
Middle Actions	second, third, fourth... then, next, after that/this following that, afterwards, later subsequently, soon, eventually
Concurrent Actions	in the meantime, meanwhile at the same time, simultaneously at this point, concurrently
Last Action	last, finally, eventually in the end

In the preceding passage, a sequencing marker is used for each of the four actions. You need to be aware, however, that markers are not always used for each action. An example of this can be found in the following passage.

The disease known as sleeping sickness is transmitted to humans by the tsetse fly, an insect found largely in parts of Africa. The cycle begins when the fly extracts blood from an infected person or animal. This blood contains a particular parasite which reproduces in the fly. These parasites subsequently find their way to the fly's salivary glands. When the tsetse fly finds another victim, the disease is passed on.

Locate the marker, if any, used in each action. If no marker was used, put an "X" in the space.

action 1: _____

action 2: _____

action 3: _____

action 4: _____

When an author wants to arrange items in a list, words called **enumeration markers** can be used. Table 4.2 identifies many of these markers. You will notice that many enumeration markers can also be used as sequencing markers. In the following passage, find the markers that enumerate a list.

All electronic computers have certain components in common. The first one is an input device through which raw data are fed. A storage capacity or memory is also necessary. The function of this component is to hold the inputted data for subsequent use or retrieval. Third is an accumulator or arithmetic unit, used for computations and problem-solving. Next is a control unit which accepts and carries out instructions. The final component is an output device through which the results arrive.

total number of components: _____

Which enumeration markers are used?

_____   _____   _____

_____   _____

TABLE 4.2: Enumeration Markers

Items Listed In No Special Order	Beginning Position	first, first of all in the first place to begin, to start initially
	Middle Position	another, next second, third... in the second place furthermore, moreover in addition, also
	End Position	the other, finally last but not least to conclude (with) last
Items Listed In Order of Importance	Important Items First	first and foremost first and most importantly
	Important Items Last	above all on top of it all far more importantly last and most importantly

In the preceding passage, all the items in the list are equally important. Items often vary in importance, however. Sometimes the author puts the most important items first and the least important ones last. Occasionally, the author does the opposite. Examine the following passage, taken from sociology.

> What conditions are needed for a panic? First and foremost, the situation must be perceived to be threatening. Next, the solution to this crisis must be to escape fast. Third, the opportunites for successful escape as well as adequate time must be seen as limited. Panics happen when it is difficult for most people to escape.

total number of conditions

necessary for a panic: _____

In what order are the conditions mentioned?

_____ no particular order

_____ most to least important

_____ least to most important

Which enumeration markers are used?

_____   _____   _____

4.2 Exemplifying and Specifying Markers

One group of markers will show you when an example is coming. Table 4.3 contains two types of **exemplifying markers**: those which introduce typical or representative examples; and those which introduce important or significant examples. In the following two sentences, decide which marker introduces a typical example and which introduces an important one.

_____   Precious metals, in particular gold, either exist in very limited quantities or are extremely difficult to mine.

_____   Precious metals, such as gold and silver, either exist in very limited quantities or are extremely difficult to mine.

Find the exemplifying marker in the following passage, taken from psychology.

Colors do not evoke the same reactions throughout the world. In Japan, for instance, red is associated with danger, while in China it is linked to feelings of happiness and joy. Even within cultures, feelings about colors can vary widely.

Which marker is used? _____

Which kind of marker is it?   typical   important

How many examples are given? _____

TABLE 4.3: Exemplifying Markers

Markers for Typical Examples	for example, for instance including, as follows such as, e.g., for one to illustrate this by way of example a case in point, say
Markers for Important Examples	especially, notably, mostly particularly, in particular mainly, chiefly, principally

An author can make a difficult point clearer to you in two ways. One way is by stating the point again using different words. The second way is by identifying all of the parts of the point. Table 4.4 includes a group of words called **specifying markers** that can be used when an author wants to do this. Decide if the author <u>restates</u> or <u>identifies</u> in the following two sentences.

_____   Matter is not continuous; <u>that is</u>, it cannot be subdivided without limit.

_____   The sun is the ultimate source of all the major elements of erosion (<u>i.e.</u>, streams, winds, waves, and glaciers).

TABLE 4.4: Specifying Markers

Markers to Restate a Point	i.e., that is in other words put differently
Markers to Identify the Components of a Point	namely, i.e. that is to say specifically

A special way of specifying items is through the use of the word respectively. This word means "in the order mentioned." Look at the use of this word in the following sentences.

The prefixes "macro" and "micro" come from Greek words that mean "large" and "small" respectively.

macro = _____   micro = _____

The planet closest to the Sun is Venus. The next closest are Mercury and Earth respectively.

_____ is closest, followed by _____ ,

and then _____ .

4.3 Detouring and Resuming Markers

Markers in this group (see Table 4.5) show when an author is (1) departing from the main points of the reading or (2) returning to the main points again. Consider the example below.

> Vitamins are organic compounds necessary to human life. Indeed, the prefix **vita–** means "life." In spite of extensive clinical information concerning vitamin deficiencies, the exact biological role they play is unclear. The first instance of vitamin-related diseases, incidentally, was recorded by the British navy before 1800. It was noticed that those sailors whose diets included lime and lemon juice were unaffected by scurvy, a condition now known to be caused by a lack of Vitamin C. Fruit juice soon thereafter became a standard ration on board all British ships, and British sailors became known as "limeys." To return to the previous point, although the role of vitamins remains largely unknown, researchers have been able to identify all of the major ones. In the following paragraphs, each will be examined.

detouring marker: _____

resuming marker: _____

TABLE 4.5: Detouring and Resuming Markers

Detouring Markers	incidentally, parenthetically by the way to digress for a moment
Resuming Markers	to resume getting back to the argument to return to the previous point to get back to the issue at hand

4.4 Concluding Markers

A conclusion can be of two kinds. In the first type, the author briefly repeats the main points of the preceding paragraphs. Here, nothing new is added. In the second type, the author tells you what the information in the preceding paragraphs suggests or implies. Here, the conclusion is the final step in a chain of reasoning, and the author takes a position based on the facts presented.

Both types of conclusions can be signaled by markers, examples of which are found in Table 4.6. Read the following two passages and decide which type of conclusion is used.

It is axiomatic that sleep is necessary for humans because the body requires rest. Though scientists have long wondered why sleep is essential, little evidence has as yet surfaced. It appears that under normal circumstances the body uses roughly the same amount of energy when asleep as when awake. In short, the reasons for sleep remain a mystery.

Which concluding marker is used? _____

What type of conclusion does this marker signal?

_____ brief review of previous information

_____ position taken

Blood can be classified into types: A, B, AB, and O. Each person has only one of these four types. Wide statistical research on the distribution of these types showed some surprising results. A majority of the original native population in any area of the world has the same blood type. Based on these distributions, researchers have therefore been able to propose models of human movement.

Which concluding marker is used? _____

What type of conclusion does this marker signal?

_____ brief review of previous information

_____ position taken

TABLE 4.6: Concluding Markers

Markers to Review Previous Points	in summary, to summarize to sum up, to review to recap, to recapitulate to reiterate in short, in a word in brief, briefly to conclude, in conclusion on the whole, all in all in all, in essence
Markers to Form a Concluding Opinion	therefore, thus, then you can deduce/infer from... to conclude, in conclusion given (all) these points

4.5 Cause and Effect Markers

Markers in this group show that one action brings about another (see Section 3.4). The relationship between these two actions can be expressed by using any of a large number of **cause and effect markers** (see Table 4.7). The actions in the following two sentences might be causally connected. Which is the cause and which is the effect?

_____ Temperatures dropped below freezing.

_____ The crops died.

A sentence expressing a causal relationship between these two actions may introduce the cause first and then identify the effect, or vice versa. In the four sentences which follow, decide if the order is <u>cause to effect</u> or <u>effect to cause</u>.

_____ The crops died because of freezing temperatures.

_____ As a consequence of freezing temperatures, the crops died.

_____ Owing to freezing temperatures, the crops died.

_____ The reason the crops died was freezing temperatures.

TABLE 4.7: Cause and Effect Markers

Cause Markers	because, since, as, for because of, owing to, due to the result of, to result from the consequence of the effect of ___ on ___
Effect Markers	as a result, as a consequence therefore, thus, consequently hence, accordingly, the cause of the reason for, to result in for fear that, on the grounds that

4.6 Purpose Markers

A special set of words (see Table 4.8) shows that a particular effect or result is intended or hoped for. These words do not show that the effect actually happened. They answer the question "Why?" Examine the use of **purpose markers** in the following sentence.

Company A dropped prices in order to sell more products.

Why were prices cut?_____

Did Company A sell more products after taking this action?

_____

Quite frequently, the marker used in the preceding example is reduced, leaving only <u>to</u> followed by a verb.

Company A dropped prices to sell more products.
To sell more products, Company A dropped prices.

TABLE 4.8: Purpose Markers

so that, for the purpose of
in order to, in order that
for the (simple) reason that

4.7 Comparison Markers

Markers in this group, shown in Table 4.9, will indicate similarities and differences between two or more things. Examine the comparisons made in the following passage, taken from chemistry.

Under the right circumstances, a solid can become a liquid. Although the chemical properties of a particular substance do not change, some of the physical properties may. For instance, a solid will evaporate extremely slowly, whereas a liquid's rate of evaporation is relatively quick. The two states do share certain likenesses. Most noticeably, both a solid and a liquid can be seen and felt.

number of things compared: _____

markers showing similarity: _____

_____

markers showing difference: _____

_____

In the preceding passage, one thing was compared with one other thing (X is compared to Y). Other combinations are possible, for instance:

(A + B) is compared to (C + D)
A is compared to (B + C)

A passage illustrating one of these combinations follows.

Under the right circumstances, a substance can exist as either a solid, a liquid or a gas. With respect to physical properties, solids and liquids are quite dissimilar to gases. The latter cannot be seen unless colored. In addition, gases are highly compressible and can change volume.

What are compared? _____

marker showing difference: _____

number of differences: _____

TABLE 4.9: Comparison Markers

Similarity Markers	similarly, likewise alike, similar to, likeness the same as, both, neither
Contrast Markers	in contrast, by way of contrast on the other hand, conversely instead, unlike, dissimilar although, though, even though whereas, while, but, yet,

4.8 Reinforcing and Opposition Markers

Reinforcing markers introduce an additional idea while opposition markers introduce an idea that goes against or counters another idea. Both types are listed in Table 4.10. In the following passage, try to locate these markers.

The thermal pollution entering the water supply comes from electric power generation as well as other industrial processes. Heat changes water by reducing the oxygen content. This, of course, negatively affects marine life. Despite this, it may be that the advantages of thermal pollution outweigh the disadvantages. For instance, warm temperatures are helpful in the development of fish eggs.

reinforcing marker: _____

opposition marker: _____

TABLE 4.10: Reinforcing and Opposition Markers

Reinforcing Markers	as well, also, and in addition, furthermore moreover, besides what is more
Opposition Markers	although, even though in spite of, despite notwithstanding nonetheless, nevertheless but ___ anyway but ____ still yet ____ still

4.9 Subject Clauses

That a sentence having a long clause as its subject is difficult to understand is well known. Did you have a problem understanding that sentence? If so, the next paragraph will help.

In order to make sense of sentences with subject clauses, you should first identify the main verb, and then make a question by putting the word "what" in front of it. The answer to the question is the subject clause. Let us examine the first sentence of this section.

What is well known? That a sentence having a long
subject is difficult to understand.

Table 4.11 identifies various sentence types with subject clauses. For each of the examples in the table, find the main verb and underline it, and then put parentheses around the subject clause. The first one is done for you.

TABLE 4.11: Subject Clauses

Type	Example
(That + sentence) + main verb + xxxxxx	(That business owners and managers rely heavily on banks and other lending institutions for capital funds) <u>is</u> one reason why these lenders are able to influence business policy.
(For ___ to ____) + main verb + xxxxxx	For scientists to take the position that they bear no responsibility for the uses to which their inventions are put might come as a shock to some people.
	For people not to heed the lessons of history is an invitation to repeat past mistakes.
(To _____) + main verb + xxxxxx	To subscribe to the notion that science need not be based on experimental observations and quantitative measurements strikes many of us as odd.
(Possessive + V-ing) + main verb + xxxxx	The U.S. government's deregulating of the airline industry a few years ago in the wake of overwhelming public support has permitted airlines operating domestically to add profitable routes and discontinue uneconomical ones.
	The surgeon general's not including the effects of smoking in the annual report led to speculation that the tobacco industry had applied political pressure.
(Possessive + noun)	The general's order to attack the enemy without first knowing the strength of the enemy cost him not only the battle, but probably the war.
(Wh- + Sentence) + main verb + xxxxx	How the problem of chronic food shortages in needy countries is to be solved is the subject of a survey of the Food and Agricultural Organization of the United Nations.
	Where this line of inquiry might go cannot be known in advance.

4.10 Unusual Word Order

Were all sentences written using the same word order, the effect on you would be one of boredom. This is why authors choose from a variety of sentence types. The first sentence in this paragraph, for instance, normally would be written as follows:

If all sentences were written using the same word order, the effect on you would be one of boredom.

When you saw that the first sentence above started with a verb, you probably expected a question. This expectation perhaps caused confusion when you discovered the sentence was not a question after all. In Table 4.12, you will find some other sentence types that may be sources of reading difficulty.

TABLE 4.12: Inversion

Type	Example
Conditional Expressions	<u>Were</u> Newton alive today, he would doubtless be pleased to know that his theories governing the movement of planets are still accepted. (= <u>If</u> Newton <u>were</u> alive today,...)
	<u>Had</u> the battle been lost, the whole course of history might have changed. (= <u>If</u> the battle <u>had</u> been lost,...)
	<u>Should</u> present means of storing nuclear waste prove inadequate, new ones will surely be devised. (= <u>If</u> present means of storing nuclear waste <u>should</u> prove inadequate,...)
Expressions Indicating Location	<u>Along the edge of the river</u> were placed sand bags. (= Sandbags were placed along the edge of the river.)
	<u>At the very top of the mountain</u> stands an observatory. (= An observatory stands at the very top of the mountain.)
Other Instances	Just as interesting was the second study. (= The second study was just as interesting.)
	Unexpectedly from the rear came troops loyal to the government. (= The troops loyal to the government came unexpectedly from the rear.)

4.11 Supplementive Constructions

This type of sentence being a frequent cause of reading difficulty, it is included in this chapter. A supplementive construction is a sentence with two related ideas. The first idea tells you <u>why</u> or <u>when</u> the second idea happens. Read the first sentence in this paragraph again and answer the following question.

Why is this type of sentence studied in this chapter?

Because it is _____

Table 4.13 provides additional examples of supplementive constructions. Notice how the verb form in the first half of the sentence changes.

TABLE 4.13: Supplementive Constructions

Type	Example (followed by informal version)
Active Verbs	The rate of population growth being much greater than ever before, many social scientists are concerned with how governments will cope with this problem.
	The rate of population growth is much greater than ever before. This is why many social scientists are concerned with how governments will cope with this problem.
	The experiment having ended, the results were compiled and published.
	When the experiment ended, the results were compiled and published.
Passive Verbs	The need alleviated, the problem ceased to exist.
	When the need was alleviated, the problem ceased to exist.
	The contract having been broken, the firm had no choice but to sue for damages.
	Because the contract had been broken, the firm had no choice but to sue for damages.
No Verb	The desert now an oasis, the importation of fresh fruits and vegetables will begin to decrease.
	Because the desert is now an oasis, the importation of fruits and vegetables will begin to decrease.
	The sale of the property over, the owners moved out.
	When the sale of the property was over, the owners moved out.

4.12 Shift in Grammatical Function

When you learn words, you also learn how they function grammatically. For instance, you think of *word* as a noun, and when you see or hear it, you expect it to behave like a noun. Using your knowledge of grammar, complete the following sentence:

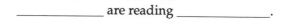

_____ are reading _____.

Quite probably, you completed this sentence by considering *are reading* as a verb, and you wrote something like: They are reading a newspaper. Some of you, however, might have considered <u>are</u> as the verb, and <u>reading</u> as an adjective. If you did, you wrote something like: Those are reading problems. Table 4.14 provides other examples of when words may take unusual or unexpected turns in grammatical function. Usually, you can tell whether a word is being used as a verb, a noun, or an adjective by reading the rest of the sentence.

TABLE 4.14: Grammatical Shifts

Type	Example
Shift to Verb	People *bank* money at local institutions. Fund distributors *market* shares and provide prospectuses. Workers *machine* the precise parts.
Shift to Noun	Two opposing forces are *thrust* and *drag*. Nose *drops* provide temporary relief from congestion. Frequent and extended eye *contact* is thought to indicate a need for affiliation.
Shift to Adjective	An integral part of buildings and bridges is *expanding* parts. Off the entrance are *living* quarters. Secure houses have *locked* doors. Phosphate-based detergents are *banned* or *restricted* products in the United States.

Summary

In this chapter, you studied a set of words called markers which help you in following the structure of a text. Markers can indicate a sequence of events, a list, specific or general examples, digressions, and conclusions. Other markers can show cause, effect, purpose, comparison, reinforcement, and opposition. We also studied a number of sentence types that can cause reading difficulties.

Recommended Reading

Coates, Marvin and Donald Pederson. 1983. *Thinking in English.* Boston: Little, Brown. See Chapter 2 on nominalizations.

Frank, Marcella. 1972. *Modern English, Part II: Sentences and Complex Structures.* Englewood Cliffs, NJ: Prentice-Hall. All chapters are useful.

Oshima, Alice and Ann Hogue. 1983. *Writing Academic English.* Reading, MA: Addison-Wesley. See Chapter 3 on transition signals (markers).

Pierson, Ruth and Susan Vik. 1987. *Making Sense in English.* Reading, MA: Addison-Wesley. All chapters are useful.

Thomson, A.J. and A.V. Martinet. 1980. *A Practical English Grammar.* Oxford: Oxford University Press. See Chapter 30 on markers.

Thought Questions

1. Explain the difference in meaning between the following two sentences. Refer to Tables 4.3 and 4.4 if necessary.

   "X" consists of several elements, namely....

   "X" consists of several elements, including....

2. Students occasionally confuse specially and especially. The former means "for a particular purpose," while the latter means "in particular." Decide which one should be used in the following sentences.

   Molecules of elements are _____ arranged to form compounds.

   Molecules are _____ important to our understanding of chemistry.

3. The following two-word verbs all are used to show casual relationships: lead to, stem from, come from, bring about. With some of them, the cause goes in front of the verb and with others it goes after it. Make a sentence for each verb.

4. The English word summary comes from the Latin word summa which means sum, a term used in the field of mathematics. Consult your dictionary and find the difference between a summary and a summation.

5. Make a list consisting of five items, placing them in order of decreasing importance. Then make a list of the same five items, placing them in order of increasing importance. What effect does each list have on the reader?

Exercises

Exercise A Examine the following passages and determine which type of conclusion is used. First locate and underline the concluding markers. Then write <u>restatement</u> if it summarizes information, or <u>determination</u> if it comes to a judgment about the information.

_____ **1.** Misunderstandings happen every day. The most frequent explanation for them is that the meaning of the message is incorrectly transmitted or received. However, human communication also has social dimensions. Even if the meaning is clear, there may be resistance or prejudice toward it. If the message carries bad or unacceptable information, an individual may not want to believe it. These, then, are several other explanations for apparent misunderstandings.

_____ **2.** We all have information about ourselves that we do not have about others. No matter how well we think we know another person, we can never know as much about that person as we do about ourselves. In perceiving ourselves, we are motivated by the need to protect our self-esteem. Thus, we may justify our own failures more readily than those of others.

_____ **3.** One of the most common ideas about sleep is that it provides rest for the body. If kept awake for long periods of time, people will eventually die. There is as yet no clear reason why this is so. The body shows no significant change in energy consumption whether asleep or awake. In short, the reasons for sleep remain mysterious.

_____ **4.** Before environments are shaped, they are conceived as ideas. By giving physical expression to these ideas, architects help establish order in the world. The structures around us, in turn, determine in part how we behave. Given this, the influence of architecture in our lives is powerful indeed.

_____ **5.** The invention of the printing press in the middle of the fifteenth century had immediate and far-reaching effects. When books were copied by hand, only a few could hope to read them. Presses made books available at prices that would not have been believed a few short years earlier. Anything written could now be relatively quickly and cheaply reproduced and distributed. One obvious conclusion from this was that learning need never again be the monopoly of a small group of people.

Exercise B Put brackets around the subject clause, and underline the main verb in each of the following sentences.

1. What is important for us to see here is that it is sometimes difficult to find the subject and verb of a sentence.

2. Whether nuclear energy provides more benefit or harm to society cannot be answered at this stage.

3. That large bubbles formed within the liquid and rose to the surface indicates that the liquid was boiling.

4. For astronauts to land on the moon in 1969 was a dramatic event in space exploration.

5. That all systems operate according to general principles, such as feedback, is certain.

6. Pasteur's linking of germs to disease made the study of bacteriology popular and advanced it to the level of a science.

7. Where the implications of the study may lead is seen as the most exciting phase of the projects.

8. Why the experiment, conducted under the best conditions, failed will probably never be known.

9. For gold to have been the international monetary standard for as long as it was attests to the value people universally assign to it.

10. Kepler's developing of the three laws that explain the motion of the planets earned him a place in astronomy texts.

Exercise C Each of the underlined words in the sentences below can be used as various parts of speech. In the space provided, write whether the underlined word is used as a noun, a verb, or an adjective.

_____ 1. Human <u>needs</u> and wants change with time.

_____ 2. Writing <u>functions</u> as a container for information.

_____ 3. <u>Damaging</u> earthquakes preceded the catastrophe and warned that the volcano was not extinct.

_____ 4. Deductive logic <u>reasons</u> from the general to the specific.

_____ 5. There are several explanations why pure competition according to supply and demand <u>functions</u> only on a limited basis in the U.S.

_____ 6. In all <u>reaches</u> of life and at all times, there has been great curiosity about this phenomenon.

_____ 7. The temperature lowering <u>effect</u> produced by the evaporation of water in a nuclear power plant is frequently used for commercial purposes.

_____ 8. There are <u>marked</u> indications that the economy is on the road to recovery.

_____ 9. Perception <u>sets</u> the individual to expect to encounter the world in a particular way.

_____ 10. Reasonable work <u>concerns</u> among management put job security at the top.

_____ 11. Steam <u>issues</u> from the mouth of the geyser before, during, and immediately after an eruption.

_____ 12. Most investment <u>flows</u> between countries, however, are channeled through multinational corporations.

_____ 13. Certain motor <u>functions</u>, such as using the jaw and tongue in speech, are controlled by the cortex.

_____ 14. Working <u>bridges</u> now number in the thousands.

_____ 15. These are <u>trying</u> times.

Exercise D Rewrite the following sentences so that the subject is followed by the verb phrase.

1. Endlessly and ruthlessly pound the waves on the shore, continuously reshaping the coastline.

   _____

   _____

   _____

2. Slowly and with a feeling of pride marched the soldiers along the boulevard.

   _____

   _____

   _____

3. Should it happen that a product fails to sell, a company can lose millions of investment dollars.

   _____

   _____

   _____

4. Had the committee not been in agreement, the meeting would have lasted much longer.

   _____

   _____

   _____

5. At the bottom of the pit sat one of the most important archaeological finds of the century.

   _____

   _____

   _____

6. Were all the facts surrounding the issue known today, the controversy would cease.

   _____

   _____

   _____

7. Painful and difficult was the decision to cut spending on these social programs.

   _____

   _____

   _____

8. The substance would not have turned to gas had the temperature not been raised.

   _____

   _____

   _____

9. The legislation will have deep social effects should it become law.

   _____

   _____

   _____

10. So long and thorough was the resulting study that it was ten years before the report was published.

    _____

    _____

Critical Reading

Study Objectives

By the end of this chapter, you should be able to:

■ distinguish between facts and opinions;

■ recognize vocabulary expressing degrees of doubt and certainty;

■ identify language that is used to make judgments; uncover assumptions and implications; evaluate an author's assertions.

When you read a textbook passage, you need to be able to pick out much more than the main ideas. Because so much information is packed into each sentence, you must be prepared to read your textbooks carefully. This chapter will help you judge and evaluate the information in your textbooks — in short, to read critically.

5.1 Facts and Opinions

Definition of facts

A **fact** is a generally-accepted statement that is based upon knowledge of the world around us. A statement is considered to be factual if we can confirm the accuracy or reality of the claim contained in the statement.

Verifiable facts

One way of doing this is by putting the statement to a test. For example, physicists will tell us that liquids expand somewhat when heated. A simple experiment will demonstrate that this is so. Because we can easily observe or measure the accuracy of this statement, we accept it as factual.

Unverifiable
facts

Some statements are considered to be facts even though we cannot test them. For instance, historians tell us that a man named Hammurabi ruled Babylon more than 3,000 years ago. Unfortunately, neither Hammurabi nor any of his contemporaries are alive today to help us confirm this statement. Nonetheless, his existence is accepted as factual because records exist that refer to him. We have no reason to doubt the accuracy of these records, and so we accept Hammurabi's existence as factual.

Facts can be altered or even discarded completely when new knowledge is uncovered. For 1,400 years, scientists thought it a fact that the earth was the center of the universe. Four hundred years ago, it was accepted as a fact that the earth as well as the other planets revolved in circular paths around the sun. A century later, it became known that the paths are elliptical.

Facts are
not final.

All facts are generally-accepted conclusions about reality. These conclusions may be based upon reason, observation, or a combination of the two. Our knowledge of the atom, for example, dates back at least to the time of Democritus, a Greek scientist who lived about 2,300 years ago. It seemed reasonable to him that any substance can be divided again and again until a point is reached at which it can be divided no further and still be the same substance. Indeed, the word <u>atom</u> comes from the Greek for "uncuttable."

However, it is only recently that we have been able to confirm the existence of the atom with the aid of the field ion microscope. Democritus arrived at this particular fact through reason and logic alone. Modern scientists accept the existence of the atom as a fact because they have direct experience in observing it.

Types of
opinions

An **opinion** is a personally held statement about the world around us. Opinions can be divided into two groups: **mere opinions** and **informed opinions**. The former group consists of statements that are based simply on personal preferences or tastes. Mere opinions differ from person to person. For example, someone may take the position that mathematics is more interesting than physics. This is a mere opinion.

On the other hand, informed opinions (also known as "educated guesses") consist of statements that can be supported by reasons or research but not by proof. For example, an architect may take the position that the best protection against earthquake damage is to be found in buildings that have flexible structures. Another architect may argue the opposite view, i.e., that buildings should be as rigid as possible. Both architects support their positions with studies, but neither one knows with certainty which position is accurate. We regard their positions as informed opinions.

See Table 5.1 for help.

Informed opinions are offered as explanations when the facts do not tell the whole story. Distinguishing between facts and opinions is an essential part of critical reading. Fortunately, the author often helps you by using language that expresses uncertainty. Examine the following passage, taken from astronomy.

> When stars come into existence, their surface temperatures generally range from a high of over 25,000 degrees Celsius to less than 1,000 degrees Celsius. They quickly expand to become red subgiant stars. They then are thought to enter a phase where they pulsate before contracting to become white dwarf stars. Taking several million years to cool, they finally become dark stars.

word indicating an opinion: _____

Opinions need support in order to be accepted or believed. We might accept an opinion if it seems reasonable to us or simply if an expert supports that opinion. In the latter case, you must be careful not to depend too much on the opinion of one expert. If the opinion has broad support, the author will strengthen it by mentioning several expert opinions.

TABLE 5.1: Vocabulary of Doubt and Certainty

Part of Speech	Words Suggesting Doubt	Words Suggesting Certainty
verbs	think, suppose believe, feel, seem consider, appear speculate, guess assume, surmise suggest, hypothesize propose, ponder	know, observe presume, infer ascertain determine demonstrate prove, show indicate
nouns	supposition hypothesis proposition assumption theory, appearance conjecture	law, axiom, maxim evidence, proof

adverbs	apparently, seemingly evidently, possibly probably, maybe perhaps reasonably	surely, certainly indubitably unquestionably obviously, clearly undeniably
adjectives	likely, subjective tentative, probable	objective, sure certain, clear
idioms	on the face of it to the eye	in point of fact beyond the shadow of a doubt

5.2 Judgmental Language

All of us constantly sort through information and then make decisions or judgments about it. These judgments can be divided into three types: aesthetic, ethical, and functional.

An **aesthetic judgment** is one based on beauty. For instance, you might judge the New York skyline to be beautiful, while someone else might conclude that it is ugly. When you hear words like beautiful and ugly, you know that someone is expressing a judgment. Find the words expressing aesthetic judgments in the following passage, taken from architecture.

When the Eiffel Tower was erected in Paris, local residents thought it unattractive at best and thoroughly repulsive at worst. Today, the Eiffel Tower is thought of as a splendid and elegant symbol of Paris.

words expressing positive aesthetic judgments:

_____

_____

words expressing negative aesthetic judgments:

_____

_____

A second type of judgmental language covers conclusions about morality or ethics. An **ethical judgment** involves issues of right or wrong, and good or bad. For example, when someone argues that war is wrong, an ethical judgment is reached. Consider the ethical judgments in the following passage, which comes from marketing.

Certain companies in the tobacco industry long ago irresponsibly promoted cigarette smoking as a means to control weight. In the face of pressure from consumer groups and the medical community, these companies abandoned this misleading sales approach.

words expressing ethical judgments:

_____   _____

The third kind of judgmental language covers all other types of judgments. These we will call **functional judgments**. Included are decisions about what is important, useful, acceptable, practical, and so on. For instance, after evaluating the various ways of traveling from Casablanca to Timbuctu, you might conclude that flying is fastest and easiest, but that it is also the least interesting and most costly form of transportation. Examine the judgments in the following passage, taken from art history.

> Leonardo da Vinci (1452-1519) was not only a great painter, but also a brilliant sculptor, musician, engineer, and philosopher. In short, he was one of the most talented and gifted people who ever lived.

words expressing functional judgments:

_____   _____

_____   _____

In some cases, judgments are made by the author, while in other cases the author reports judgments made by others. Look again at two of the preceding passages, and decide who is making the judgments.

Eiffel Tower: _____

da Vinci: _____

You can usually locate judgments by identifying key words, some of which are listed in Table 5.2.

TABLE 5.2: Types of Judgments

Aesthetic	Ethical	Functional
(un-)attractive	good/evil	(un-)important
beautiful/ugly	right/wrong	(in-)adequate
(un-)pleasing	(im-)moral	(un-)acceptable
(un-)appealing	(dis-)honest	(un-)fitting
plain	(im-)proper	(un-)qualified
	(ir-)responsible	(in-)appropriate
	innocent/guilty	(un-)suitable
		(un-)fitting

5.3 Assumptions

It is unnecessary and perhaps impossible for authors to include details and support for everything they write. Consider, for instance, the sentence you have just read. There is no point in spending the next few pages explaining why this statement is true. You are simply asked to assume that it is. An **assumption** is a statement which is accepted as true in the absence of proof.

As you read through a passage, you need to pay attention to the assumptions the author makes. Some assumptions are so basic that no one would have trouble accepting them. For instance, if you are reading about possible causes of cancer, you do not expect the author to prove to you that cancer exists. This is an assumption that is shared by everyone. After reading the following passage, write some of the assumptions the author expects you to accept.

In countries where protein-rich diets are rare, a form of malnutrition called kwashiorkor is common among children. This condition is characterized by disproportionately-large bellies, toneless and discolored skin, and loss of hair. In severe cases, the digestive system fails and death may occur.

_____

_____

_____

_____

_____

The conclusion reached in the passage below rests on an important assumption made by the author. Try to locate this assumption.

The population of the earth is growing at a rate of 1.8 percent each year. At this rate, the number of people inhabiting the earth will double in approximately thirty-five years.

In order for the population to double in this amount of time, what does the author assume?

_____

What factors might make this assumption incorrect?

_____

5.4 Implications

An **implication** is a thought that is indirectly suggested by something in a reading. For instance, the fact that this chapter includes a section on implications might suggest to you that this subject is important. Nowhere does the author state that it is important. You come to this conclusion on your own.

An implication may be easy to see, or it may require quite a bit of thought. Look at the following two sentences for examples of each.

> Most metals are good conductors of electricity.
> Cyprus comes from a word that means "copper."

In the first example, the choice of the word "most" suggests or implies that some metals are <u>not</u> good conductors. This implication is easy to spot. The second example implies that copper is or was found in great quantity in Cyprus. Why else would this country be so named? This conclusion requires some extra thought. In the first sentence, the implication is based upon one word only. In the second, the entire sentence carries an implication. Look at the following sentence and find the word upon which each of the two implications is based.

> Reverse osmosis is one modern process used to separate salt from water.

_____ Reverse osmosis is not the only way that salt can be extracted from water.

_____ There are methods that are older than reverse osmosis.

The implications contained in the example of reverse osmosis are both based on particular words in the sentence. In the next example, the implications are based upon the entire sentence. Decide if the implications are reasonable by writing <u>yes</u> or <u>no</u> beside them.

> There is no oxygen on the moon.

_____ Life as we know it cannot exist there.

_____ There are other gases.

In this example, you should have marked <u>yes</u> for the first and <u>no</u> for the second. Of course, it might be that there are indeed gases other than oxygen on the moon. However, there is nothing in the example that suggests that this is so. You need to make a distinction between a sentence that implies something and a sentence that simply leaves open the possibility of something. In the following sentence, decide which statement is an <u>implication</u> and which is only a <u>possibility</u>.

No country in the world has an adequate supply of all mineral resources.

_____ A country in need of a particular mineral will have to engage in trade with another country to get it.

_____ Some countries have an adequate supply of certain mineral resources.

Implications can also be made at the paragraph level. The next passage is followed by four statements. Decide if they are reasonable implications or not by writing <u>yes</u> or <u>no</u> beside them.

Biologists studying sleep have concluded that it makes little difference whether a person habitually sleeps during the day or during the night. What does seem to matter is any disturbance in an established sleep cycle.

_____ People should go to sleep and get up at regular times.

_____ Employees whose work schedules frequently alternate from day to night shift can do their jobs at maximum efficiency.

_____ Workers should accept schedules which frequently alternate from day to night hours.

_____ Travelers should consider taking flights that do not disturb sleep cycles.

5.5 Degrees of Generalization

A **generalization** is a statement about a whole class of things based upon observed members of that class. Suppose that a scientist observes that every time heat is applied to water, the temperature of the water increases. The same experiment is conducted with many liquids, each time with the same result. This, then, might lead the scientist to conclude the following: When heat is applied to a liquid, a change in temperature takes place.

Now, let us suppose that during the course of more experiments, our scientist notices that when a particular liquid reaches its boiling point, the liquid begins to change to a gas. Even when more heat is applied, no change in temperature occurs. This observation forces a change in the original generalization to the following: When heat is applied to a liquid, a change in temperature <u>usually</u> takes place. Words like <u>usually</u>, which show how often something happens, can restrict a generalization. Other frequency words are given below.

all	many	some	few	no/none
always	usually	sometimes	seldom	never

100% $\longrightarrow$ $\longrightarrow$ 0%

Many of the frequency words above can be further defined by placing the following words in front of them: nearly, very, almost.

nearly/almost + all/no/none/always/never
         very + many/few

5.6   Evaluating an Author's Assertions

An **assertion** is a statement that an author wants readers to accept. Examples of types of assertions are generalizations, conclusions, positions, and ideas. Critical readers need to analyze these assertions in order to decide how reasonable they are. One way of doing this is by examining how much supporting information an author provides for a particular assertion. The more support an author supplies, the stronger the assertion is. Compare the following two studies.

Study #1 When three cats were given a choice of pure water or slightly salted water, all of them chose to drink the salt water. From this study, we can conclude that animals prefer to eat foods containing this essential nutrient.

Study #2 When fifty cats were given a choice of pure water or slightly salted water, nearly all of them chose to drink the salt water. The same result was observed using fifty samples from various other animals. From these studies, we can conclude that animals prefer to eat foods containing this essential nutrient.

The conclusion reached in the second study is much stronger because (1) the number of cats involved in the experiment was larger, and (2) the experiment tested other animals as well. Although the conclusion in both studies is the same, the second researcher has a firmer basis than the first for reaching it.

In addition to making sure that the quantity of supporting information is adequate, you also should consider the quality of this support. One way of doing this is by checking to see if the support for the assertion is up to date. Another way is by checking to see how typical or representative the support is. Look at the following study.

In 1965, a medical examination of ten thousand adults in New York City revealed an unacceptably high level of cholesterol in their blood. This study suggests that Americans should alter their diets.

The assertion that Americans should change their eating habits cannot be reached on the strength of this study. There are at least three reasons for this. First, the study was conducted many years ago. Second, the study only tested adults and not Americans of all ages. Third, the sampling was done only in one city.

Most assertions are presented without including information about the quantity and quality of the supporting information. When this happens, critical readers should look for other ways that authors strengthen their assertions. Look at the following example, taken from marketing.

Where people live will affect how people purchase goods. People who live in rural areas buy more things through mail-order catalogs than people who live in urban areas. The reasons for this are several: rural areas have fewer shops, the shops have a smaller range of goods, and they are often inconvenient to travel to.

How does the author strengthen the assertion that people who live in rural areas make more purchases through mail-order catalogs than people in urban areas?

_____

_____

Summary

In this chapter, you examined ways of reading critically, in particular how to distinguish a fact from an opinion, how to know when judgments are being made, how to uncover assumptions and implications, and how to evaluate assertions.

Key Vocabulary

assertion	fact	implication
assumption	generalization	opinion

Recommended Reading

Adler, Mortimer J. 1978. *Aristotle for Everybody.* New York: Macmillan. See Chapter 17 on arguments.

Annis, David B. 1974. *Techniques of Critical Reasoning.* Columbus, OH: Charles E. Merrill Publishing. See Chapter 1 on the nature of logic.

Brooks, Cleanth and Robert Penn Warren. 1979. *Modern Rhetoric.* New York: Harcourt Brace Jovanovich. See Chapter 4 and Appendix B on arguments.

Thought Questions

1. Read the definition of a generalization again. Now, think of a moral principle such as, "Killing is wrong." How does this generalization differ from other types of generalizations, such as those expressing physical laws?

2. Write a paragraph that includes a mere opinion, an informed opinion, and a fact.

3. Which type of judgmental language always involves people? Explain why this is so.

4. Generalizations can be made by accumulating data through laboratory experiments, general observations, surveys/questionnaires, and case histories. In which types of textbooks would you expect to find these used?

5. Two words which are frequently confused are <u>imply</u> and <u>infer</u>. Look up the meaning of the latter and explain the difference between them. Use an example as part of your explanation.

6. Cervante's storybook hero, Don Quixote, claimed that "Facts are the enemy of truth." Explain what this means.

Exercises

Exercise A For each of the following statements write <u>fact</u> or <u>opinion</u> in the blank. Then underline the words that are used to indicate facts or opinions. If necessary, refer to Table 5.1 for help. The first one is done for you.

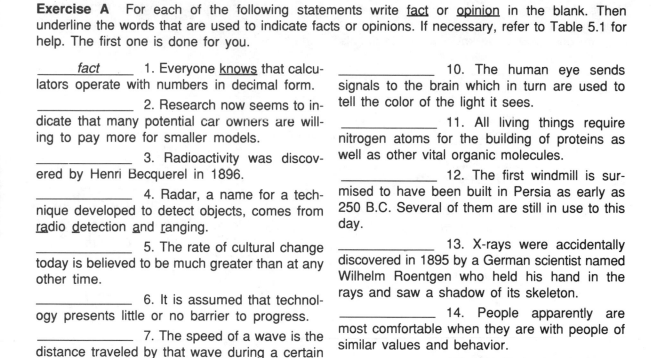

_____*fact*_____ 1. Everyone <u>knows</u> that calculators operate with numbers in decimal form.

_____ 2. Research now seems to indicate that many potential car owners are willing to pay more for smaller models.

_____ 3. Radioactivity was discovered by Henri Becquerel in 1896.

_____ 4. Radar, a name for a technique developed to detect objects, comes from <u>r</u>adio <u>d</u>etection <u>a</u>nd <u>r</u>anging.

_____ 5. The rate of cultural change today is believed to be much greater than at any other time.

_____ 6. It is assumed that technology presents little or no barrier to progress.

_____ 7. The speed of a wave is the distance traveled by that wave during a certain interval of time divided by that interval of time.

_____ 8. It has been determined that cosmic rays are constantly bombarding the earth's atmosphere.

_____ 9. It appears that species other than humans have highly-developed languages.

_____ 10. The human eye sends signals to the brain which in turn are used to tell the color of the light it sees.

_____ 11. All living things require nitrogen atoms for the building of proteins as well as other vital organic molecules.

_____ 12. The first windmill is surmised to have been built in Persia as early as 250 B.C. Several of them are still in use to this day.

_____ 13. X-rays were accidentally discovered in 1895 by a German scientist named Wilhelm Roentgen who held his hand in the rays and saw a shadow of its skeleton.

_____ 14. People apparently are most comfortable when they are with people of similar values and behavior.

_____ 15. It is likely that both personality and the environment interact to shape behavior.

Exercise B Many of the following statements contain judgmental language. Locate these words and underline them. Refer to Table 5.2 if you need help. The first one is done for you.

1. One of <u>the most significant</u> developments in the understanding of the atom was provided by Ernest Rutherford in 1911.

2. Many psychologists have found non-verbal behavior to be among the most interesting means of communicating.

3. Experiments conducted over a hundred years ago showed that chemical change could be caused by the passage of electricity through water containing chemical compounds.

4. It is not sufficient to examine living things in terms of their components. Rather, the whole organism must be examined.

5. The teakwood and mahogany doors of many traditional houses in the Al-Hasa region of Saudi Arabia are quite elaborately decorated.

6. The waste of limited resources is clearly wrong because by definition these resources cannot be replaced.

7. There are many problems associated with the combustion engine, primarily the containing of the burning flame.

8. Glass is a rather marvelous substance because it is hard yet transparent, permitting light to pass through it while blocking out most radiant heat.

9. Although Hermann Rorschach was not the first person to work with inkblots as a form of psychological testing, his test has become one of the most popular.

10. Effective leadership is determined by the leader, the followers, and the situation; thus, it is erroneous to assume that any one leadership style is best.

11. Chemicals like chlorine and arsenic and metals like mercury and lead are the most dangerous to the structure of ecosystems.

12. The height of any wave is determined by the velocity and duration of the wind as well as the available surface area of the open water.

13. Copper is a particularly valuable metal to humans because it is such a good conductor of heat and electricity.

14. The Latin name for potassium, which is <u>kalium</u>, comes from an Arabic word which means <u>ashes</u>. An English word for potassium is <u>potash</u>.

15. The structure of any organization should be flexible enough to permit goals to be accomplished without major disruption to that organization.

Exercise C Underline the assertion in each of the following passages and decide if the support for it is <u>strong</u> or <u>weak</u>. The first one is done for you.

_____weak_____ **1.** Sucrose polyester (SPE) is a calorie-free fat which was patented in 1971. <u>SPE helps people to lose weight</u>. Tests on ten subjects found that after a 20-day diet which included 60 grams of SPE, the patients lost on average 8 lbs.

_____ **2.** Over twenty years ago, a woman named Kitty Genovese was stabbed to death in New York City. Thirty-eight of her neighbors watched as she was attacked three times over a 30-minute period. Not one of the witnesses came to her assistance. This incident suggests that Americans lack social responsibility.

_____ **3.** Acid rain is destroying the maple trees of Canada and northern U.S. This determination was made after an extensive ten-year study of acid rain and its effects in four Canadian provinces and eleven American states. Trees have been so heavily damaged that yields

of maple sap (used to make syrup) have been halved.

_____ **4.** Many new products fail simply because people are unable to remember their names. Interviews of 200 consumers who watched 1,800 television commercials over a 29-day period showed that fewer than one-third could remember and describe commercials promoting new products.

_____ **5.** A survey of 5,000 students across the United States found that 60% of them occasionally slept during the day. Nearly 25% claimed they slept at odd hours simply because they enjoyed it. People are able to sleep at any time if the conditions are suitable and they choose to do so.

_____ **6.** Human beings have biological clocks. This is the conclusion of researchers who studied the behavior of people who passed up to six months without time-keeping devices in the darkness of polar winters. Subjects were observed to have a regular daily cycle of eating and sleeping.

_____ **7.** Dioxin is a toxic substance which is produced when certain chemicals containing chlorine are manufactured. Many people in industrialized countries have more dioxin in their tissues than is natural. One study measured the dioxin levels of thousands of people in different parts of the world. Europeans and Americans were consistently found to have much higher levels than nationals of non-industrialized countries.

_____ **8.** The behavior of animals will help in predicting earthquakes. Five tree-dwelling chimpanzees that were kept in California for experimental purposes were observed spending an unusual amount of time on the ground just before an earthquake.

_____ **9.** Corporate managers tend to attach greater credibility to reports when these reports are in computer printout form than when they are typed — even when statements in the reports are completely absurd. This conclusion was reached after an exhaustive three-year study which included executives from many major industries in North America and Europe.

_____ **10.** In 1938, H.G. Well's *War of the Worlds* was broadcast on radio throughout the United States. A number of people who were listening to the program actually believed an invasion from Mars was occurring. Rumors of the "invasion" quickly spread and many Americans experienced confusion and panic. From this, it is clear that people are easily influenced.

Exercise D Following each of the passages below are statements containing assumptions and implications. In the blank beside each statement write <u>yes</u> if you think the assumption or implication can logically be made. Write <u>no</u> if you think it cannot. The first one is done for you.

Thomas Robert Malthus (1776-1834) wrote a book because of an ongoing argument he had with his father. The elder Malthus believed in the power of rational behavior and thought that human progress had no limits. His son, Thomas, saw the rapidly increasing population of Europe as an obstacle to human progress. In short, he believed that people multiplied more rapidly than food could be grown and that poverty and disaster, rather than progress, were unavoidable.

___*yes*___ **1.** The Malthus family lived somewhere in Europe.

_____ **2.** The elder Malthus died before his son, Thomas, knew him.

_____ **3.** The population of Europe was growing at an ever faster rate.

_____ **4.** New technology was able to meet the need for more food.

_____ **5.** Thomas Malthus probably had a large family.

Beyond our solar system and galaxy lie countless other galaxies. Each may contain thousands of millions of planets. Statistically, the possibility of life somewhere out there is rather great. Statistically, however, the possibility of knowing about such life remains quite small. This is because even light takes millions of years to travel between galaxies.

_____ **6.** A galaxy is larger than a solar system.

_____ **7.** There is only one galaxy.

_____ **8.** There is no reason to believe that life might exist on other worlds.

_____ **9.** If life exists on other planets, there is a good chance that we will learn about it.

_____ **10.** Light can travel faster than humans.

In the early 1900s, Henry Ford developed a plan for improving methods of automobile production. Until this time, the purchase of a car was out of the financial reach of most people. Ford reasoned that inefficient production techniques resulted in low output, which in turn meant high product prices. By instituting the assembly line and mass production, Ford made it possible for many people to own an automobile.

_____ **11.** Henry Ford was an adult at the beginning of this century.

_____ **12.** Ford was born a rich man.

_____ **13.** In the early 1900s, few people had automobiles because salaries were low.

_____ **14.** Ford's production techniques resulted in a greater supply of automobiles.

_____ **15.** People bought Fords because they liked the new design of the car.

Exercise E Following each of the passages below are statements containing assumptions and implications. In the blank beside each statement write <u>yes</u> if you think the assumption or implication can logically be made. Write <u>no</u> if you think it cannot.

In 1959, a New York City disc jockey named Peter Tripp stayed awake for 201 hours in order to raise money for charity. During this eight-day feat in Times Square, his behavior was observed not only by the public but also by medical doctors and psychologists.

_____ **1.** Tripp was an adult.

_____ **2.** Charities accept donations.

_____ **3.** Tripp was married.

_____ **4.** Times Square is in New York City.

_____ **5.** The doctors and psychologists were paid for their services.

_____ **6.** Staying awake for this length of time is difficult and unusual.

_____ **7.** Tripp's undertaking might have resulted in physical and mental problems.

_____ **8.** Charities were in need of money.

_____ **9.** People would donate money if Tripp could stay awake for a long time.

_____ **10.** Tripp was able to raise money for charities.

By the third day, Tripp's eyes had begun to play tricks on him. He said he saw cobwebs in his shoes and rabbits around him. On the fourth day, his mental confusion increased and he became uncontrollably excited. By the fifth day, he showed signs of paranoia. He claimed he saw a fire around him, and he accused people watching him of setting it. After one week, he was able to go on the air for his evening broadcast. Although those who observed him at this time attested that he was indeed awake, his brain waves indicated deep sleep patterns.

_____ **11.** Tripp was blind from birth.

_____ **12.** Tripp was not wearing his shoes.

_____ **13.** Tripp was the only person who saw rabbits.

_____ **14.** People were angry because Tripp accused them of lighting a fire.

_____ **15.** Tripp could still function reasonably well after seven days.

_____ **16.** Tripp delivered his broadcast from Times Square.

_____ **17.** Tripp was alone during the broadcast.

_____ **18.** The number of people listening to the broadcast was probably smaller than usual.

_____ **19.** Brain waves could be measured in the 1950s.

_____ **20.** Tripp was more psychologically than physically affected.

On the eighth day, a neurologist came to examine Tripp. The doctor carried an umbrella and wore dark clothes. Tripp assumed that the doctor was an undertaker who had come because he thought Tripp was near death. He jumped off the examining table and unsuccessfullly attempted to escape. Later that day, Tripp fell asleep and stayed that way for thirteen hours. When he awoke, he felt reasonably well.

_____ **21.** A neurologist is a type of medical doctor.

_____ **22.** The neurologist was passing through Times Square by a happy coincidence.

_____ **23.** The weather on that day was sunny.

_____ **24.** Undertakers wear dark clothes.

_____ **25.** Tripp was afraid of the neurologist.

_____ **26.** Tripp was lying down during the examination.

_____ **27.** The neurologist completed the examination.

_____ **28.** Without sleep, people cannot survive any longer than eight days.

_____ **29.** If we do not sleep at all one night, we should sleep twice as long the following night.

_____ **30.** Sleep is necessary for mental and physical well-being.

CHAPTER 6

Vocabulary

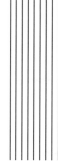

Study Objectives

By the end of this chapter, you should be able to:

- decide when it is wise to use a dictionary;
- locate appropriate definitions in a dictionary;
- apply the appropriate meaning for a group of commonly-used words;
- understand metaphoric use of language;
- recognize strategies that authors use to avoid gender bias.

6.1 When to Use a Dictionary

You can expect to meet many new words as you read through your textbooks. When this happens, you will want to reach for a dictionary. This is not always a good idea. There are three reasons why you should not depend too much on a dictionary:

1. Using a dictionary slows down your reading speed;
2. Using a dictionary can interrupt your thinking;
3. Using a dictionary is often unnecessary.

Let's examine this last point more carefully. A good reader will try to guess the meaning of a new word by analyzing the context in which it occurs. The context frequently makes the meaning of a word clear.

Did you look up <u>context</u>? If so, you are using your dictionary too much. There is enough information in the sentences above for you to guess its meaning. Put a checkmark beside the probable definition of this word.

_____ spelling   _____ situation

_____ pronunciation   _____ origin

The context might provide help in the form of synonyms and antonyms for an unfamiliar word. A synonym is a word which has roughly the same meaning as another word (see Section 7.1). Now that you know the meaning of <u>synonym</u>, you also have a fair idea of the meaning of <u>antonym</u>.

An <u>antonym</u> is a word which has the _____

meaning of another word. In fact, the word <u>antonym</u>

even has an antonym. It is the word _____.

For more practice in guessing meanings through the use of synonyms and antonyms, examine the third sentence of Chapter 2, and then the title of Chapter 4. Answer the following:

Which word has the same meaning as <u>topic</u>?	Which word means the opposite of <u>helps</u>?
_____	_____

Aside from the context, an analysis of an unfamiliar word itself can often help determine meaning. A word can sometimes be divided into parts (or elements). Each element has a meaning (See Table 6.1). By combining the meanings of these elements, you can arrive at a definition. For example, if you know that <u>fortune</u> means <u>luck</u> and that <u>mis-</u> means <u>bad</u>, then you can figure out the meaning of <u>misfortune</u>.

<u>misfortune</u> = _____

Let's try analysizing the word that is thought to be the longest word in English:

pneumonoultramicroscopicsilicovolcanoconiosis

A breakdown of this word's components is as follows:

pneumon = lungs	silico = silicon
ultra = extremely	volcano = eruption
micro = small	coni = dust
scopic = to see	osis = condition

By combining some of this word's elements, you can piece together the following definition:

A _____ of the _____ caused

when _____ _____ particles of _____ _____
are inhaled.

By now, you can see that it is often quite possible to find an approximate meaning for unfamiliar words without using a dictionary. Unfortunately, this is not always the case. Sometimes, neither the context nor an analysis of the word will help much. When this happens, you need to ask yourself two questions.

1. Is this word essential to an understanding of the reading?
2. Is this a word I have often met before but still do not know what it means?

You should use your dictionary if the answer to either of these questions is "yes."

TABLE 6.1: Common Word Elements

Meaning	Element	Example
above	hyper-	hyperactive
	super-	supersonic
across	trans-	transplant
after	post-	postdate
again	re-	reconstruct
against	anti-	antimagnetic
all	omni-	omnipresent
back	retro-	retroactive
before	pre-	premature
below	hypo-	hypodermic
between	inter-	international
cause to become	-en	harden
	-ize	sterilize
central	mid-	midpoint
direction of	-ward	homeward
extremely	ultra-	ultrasonic
false	pseudo-	pseudoscience
far	tele-	television
fear of	-phobia	hydrophobia
first/earliest	proto-	protohistory
for/forward	pro-	proceed
former	ex-	ex-president

half	semi-	semiarid
irritation of	-itis	appendicitis
killer	-cide	bactericide
large	macro-	macronucleus
less than usual	under-	underweight
love of	-phile	hydrophile
	phil-	philanthropy
many	multi-	multisensory
	poly-	polychromatic
more than usual	extra-	extraordinary
	over-	oversleep
new	neo-	neonatal
not	a-	asymmetrical
	in-	indivisible
	non-	nonmetallic
	un-	unbroken
opposite	counter-	counterattack
resembling	quasi-	quasistellar
self	auto-	autobiography
small	micro-	microfilm
someone who	-ant	occupant
	-er	teacher
	-ist	physicist
study of	-logy	psychology
together	co-	copilot
too little	under-	underestimate
too much	over-	overpay
under	sub-	subterranean
water	aqua-	aquarium
	hydro-	hydroelectric
without	-less	weightless
wrong	mal-	maladjusted
	mis-	misunderstand

6.2 Technical Vocabulary

People in a particular profession will use words that are known only to other people in the same field of study. This specialized vocabulary is called **technical vocabulary.**

A word may have general <u>and</u> technical definitions. For example, <u>work</u> is commonly thought to mean "any physical or mental effort." A physics text, however, will state that work is performed only when something is forced to move. So, if you push against a brick wall, are you doing work?

a physicist would answer: yes   no

most people would answer: yes   no

When a word has both general and technical meanings, the author will probably tell you which definition is used in your textbook. The following example illustrates this.

> Water pollution means different things to different people. To some, it means the presence of toxic chemicals and to others it means the presence of disease-carrying bacteria. To many scientists, however, water pollution is suggested by the presence of waste materials composed largely of carbon, hydrogen, and nitrogen.

general: presence of _____ or _____

technical: presence of _____

A single concept may be expressed by several different technical words, each one used in a different field. The underlined words in the three sentences below all mean "an estimate of coming events or conditions." Match the sentence with the appropriate field.

_____ 1. meteorology

_____ 2. medicine

_____ 3. most other fields

a. A patient's <u>prognosis</u> can be made only after a careful physical examination.

b. A <u>forecast</u> of general weather patterns is always easier to make than one of day-to-day changes in the weather.

c. Any <u>prediction</u> of how well buildings can withstand an earthquake must take into account a large number of factors.

Fortunately, you will not have to know most technical vocabulary before you read your textbooks. When specialized terms are introduced, they are usually printed in boldface or italics (see Section 2.4) along with their definitions. Many textbooks also have glossaries (see Section 1.6) to help you understand technical vocabulary.

6.3 Formal Vocabulary

The words you choose to use when in one situation may differ greatly from the words you choose in another situation. This is because certain words that are appropriate for one particular occasion will not be appropriate for another. For example, think of an occasion when you would say, "Hi" and one when you would say, "Good day."

"Hi." _____

"Good day." _____

In both cases, the message is fundamentally the same: you are greeting someone. However, the former is more casual and informal, while the latter is more serious, dignified, and formal. Whether you are speaking or whether you are writing, your choice of words will depend on the situation.

In general, the language used in textbooks is rather formal. Compare the following two passages, both of which communicate the same message, and decide which is more likely to be included in a textbook.

Malaria is found everywhere. People and also different kinds of monkeys, rats, birds, and even snakes can get this sickness.

Malaria has a worldwide distribution. Not only human beings, but also various species of monkeys, rats, birds, and even snakes can contract this malady.

The passage on the right includes several examples of formal vocabulary, and is therefore more likely to be found in a textbook. Find the formal vocabulary from this passage and complete the following:

found everywhere = _____

different = _____

kinds = _____

get = _____

this sickness = _____

Formal vocabulary may present a problem to you at first. In time, however, you will acquire a sufficient number of these lexical items to comprehend any textbook. Put informally, you will pick up enough of these words to be able to understand any textbook.

acquire   =   _____

sufficient   =   _____

lexical items   =   _____

comprehend   =   _____

6.4 Finding the Right Definition

Suppose you come across a word that is essential to an understanding of the passage, but you have no idea what this word means. The context is no help. You have searched the glossary and the index (see Section 1.9), but your word is not there. You decide to turn to the dictionary, but you discover that many definitions are listed. Which one do you choose?

The first step is to identify which part of speech your word is. This is important because a definition may change greatly from one part of speech to another, as in the following:

1. The <u>fare</u> was raised in order to meet operating costs.

   a charge for transportation; food or drink

2. The world economy is expected to <u>fare</u> much better in the next decade.

   to happen; to get along

As you can see, the definition of <u>fare</u> the noun is quite different from <u>fare</u> the verb. Even within a part-of-speech group, there may be various definitions. Is there a way to shorten this search? Read on.

If your word has a special meaning to the field you are studying, then the dictionary often identifies this meaning as belonging to that subject. Dictionaries do this by using field labels. A field label identifies the special area (e.g., chemistry, biology, music) to which the definition applies. Match the three definitions below of <u>operation</u> with the appropriate field label: <u>medicine</u>, <u>computer science</u>, and <u>mathematics</u>.

_____: A procedure for repairing an injury in a living body, especially one performed by doctors using instruments

_____: A process such as addition or substitution performed in a fixed sequence

_____: An action that results from one command

6.5 Familiar Yet Confusing Words

Familiar words are sometimes responsible for more miscomprehension than unfamiliar ones. This can happen when you read a word which has several meanings and you apply the wrong one. For example, the title of this section contains the word yet. More frequently, this word means "up to this time," as in the sentence:

This lesson is not finished yet.

Perhaps you applied this meaning when you first read the section title. However, this meaning makes no sense in this context. Refer to Table 6.2 to find the correct meaning of yet in this context.

yet = _____

TABLE 6.2: High Frequency Words With Multiple Meanings

Word	Meaning	Example
as	because	As the building design is flexible, it is not too late to change it.
	in the same manner	She conducted the test exactly as before.
	while/when	As the solution boiled, the chemical change occurred.
	for example	Halogens, as fluorine and bromine, are never found free in nature.
	in the capacity of	Television as an instrument of education is an important social force.

but	however	The goods were manufactured <u>but</u> not marketed.
	other than/ with the exception of	Scientists respect nothing <u>but</u> the facts.
for	because/ on the grounds that	They had to stop <u>for</u> the hour was late.
	in spite of	<u>For</u> all his efforts, his work was recognized only after he died.
however	on the other hand	Some firms offer a variety of services; others, <u>however,</u> specialize in just one or two.
	in whatever manner or way	<u>However</u> much he tried, he failed.
just	perhaps/ possibly	The health of the ecomony <u>just</u> may depend on factors such as these.
	precisely/ exactly	There was <u>just</u> enough heat to cause an explosion.
	only	A reaction <u>just</u> means that the test worked.
	a short time ago	She has <u>just</u> finished writing her bibliography.
	right, fair	A <u>just</u> decision is the aim of every judge and jury.
now	at the present time	<u>Now</u> is a good time to invest in a computer.
	at this point in a series of events	By 9:00, the patient was anesthetized. The doctors were <u>now</u> ready to begin the operation.
	because	<u>Now</u> that the experiments are finished, the results can be published.

once	at a time in the past	<u>Once</u> there were houses on this site.
	when	<u>Once</u> used, it will be gone.
	one time	Disposable items, such as paper plates, are designed to be used <u>once</u> and then thrown away.
only	however/but	The product is well-made, <u>only</u> its cost is too high.
	simply/ merely	This is <u>only</u> one of the many reasons why this process is preferred.
	alone in kind/sole	Iron is not the <u>only</u> metal that corrodes.
or	alternative	Certain species must be protected <u>or</u> they will become extinct.
	synonymous or equivalent expression	Tornadoes <u>or</u> twisters are smaller and more intense than most other storms.
	approximation or indefiniteness	A cure cannot be expected for at least a decade <u>or</u> two.
since	because	<u>Since</u> the experiments are to be repeated, a standard must be defined.
	from the time	<u>Since</u> the early 1980s, scientists have learned a great deal about AIDS in particular and viral diseases in general.
so	consequently	The results were inconclusive and <u>so</u> we must try again.
	in the same way/ likewise	Graphite represents a pure form of carbon and <u>so</u> do diamonds.

still	up to the present time	New products are <u>still</u> test-marketed.
	nevertheless	Smoking is indisputably linked to cancer. <u>Still,</u> some people refuse to accept the evidence.
	quiet/ not moving	Though the water was <u>still,</u> it was not stagnant.
then	after that	Newton rejected Galileo's theories of motion and <u>then</u> formulated his own.
	at another time	The United Nations was formed in 1945. Even <u>then,</u> it had a large membership.
	consequently	An atom is the smallest particle of an element that can exist and still have the properties of that element. The atom, <u>then,</u> is the building block for all substances.
while	as long as/ during the time that	<u>While</u> the solution was boiling, the chemical reaction took place.
	although	<u>While</u> lead is a poor heat conductor, copper is a good one.
yet	but/ despite this	They expected the experiment to fail, <u>yet</u> they tried it again.
	thus far/ up to a certain time	Although the medicine was successful with laboratory animals, the government was not <u>yet</u> ready to approve its use on humans.
	in addition/ still	There is <u>yet</u> another school of management to be discussed.

6.6 Metaphoric Language

Authors sometimes compare elements of a familiar experience with those of an unfamiliar one in order to increase the reader's understanding of a text. For example, in describing the effect of a laser treatment on an imperfect diamond, an author might say that the laser "heals" the flaw. Normally, this word is reserved for living things. A sick person (and not a flawed diamond) is "healed." Examine another example here:

> Most meteors travel faster than the earth and in the same direction. A collision occurs when the "front end" of the meteor gently hits the "rear bumper" of the Earth.

Obviously, a meteor has no "front end" and the earth has no "rear bumper." What does?

_____

  Metaphoric terms are sometimes enclosed in quotation marks, as in the previous examples, and are therefore rather easy to spot. Others, however, may be more difficult to recognize:

> An economy is said to suffer from galloping inflation when prices rise by 50% or more annually.

> Which word suggests a horse running at top speed?

_____

> The profits were wiped out because the products did not sell well.

> What words suggest an eraser cleaning a blackboard?

> Expectations soared owing to the new discovery.

> What does <u>soared</u> suggest? _____

6.7 Gender Neutral Vocabulary

Until recently, masculine forms, such as <u>he</u> and <u>him</u>, were generally used when authors referred to all people (i.e., both males and females). However, most authors now avoid this practice. Table 6.3 illustrates several ways authors do this.

TABLE 6.3: Gender Bias and Neutrality

Previous Style	New Style
A good pyschologist is one who is responsive to his patient's needs.	A good psychologist is one who is responsive to his or her patient's needs.
In order to understand the problem fully, it is desirable for the subject to put himself in the the other person's shoes.	In order to understand the problem fully, it is desirable for the subject to put him- or herself in the other person's shoes.
A historian tries to record events as objectively as he can.	A historian tries to record events as objectively as s/he can.
Anyone who accepts that theory will find that there is little support for his position.	Anyone who accepts that theory will find that there is little support for their position.
A miner spends half his life underground.	Miners spend half their lives underground.

Texts sometimes alternate between masculine and feminine pronouns. The first few times you read passages written in this way, you will probably be confused. Consider the following.

Someone who suffers from a neurosis is not greatly impaired in her behavior. That is to say that her behavior is frequently rational, but at times she acts in ways that may be viewed as irrational. The particular symptoms of a neurosis may change from time to time, but usually certain patterns of behavior can be observed. This pattern can reveal important information about the person and his problem.

The effort to avoid gender bias extends to nouns as well. Words which are built around the word man are now either reduced altogether or are replaced with a gender neutral word like human or person, for example:

mankind	humankind
man-hour	person-hour
chairman	chair or chairperson
fireman	firefighter
policeman	police officer
stewardess	flight attendant

Summary

In this chapter, you studied strategies for determining the meaning of unfamiliar words with and without the use of a dictionary. You also examined a group of familiar words having multiple meanings and ways that authors use metaphoric language. Finally, you saw how authors avoid gender bias in their writing.

Key Vocabulary

field label
metaphoric language

Recommended Reading

Eisenberg, Anne. 1978. *Reading Technical Books.* Englewood Cliffs, NJ: Prentice-Hall. See Chapter 11 on technical vocabulary.

Kimmelman, Joan et al. 1984. *Reading and Study Skills.* New York: Macmillan. See Chapter 12 on dictionary use and Chapter 13 on context clues.

Levine, Adina et al. 1985. *Build it Up.* New York: Macmillan. See Chapter 3 and 4 on vocabulary.

Rosenthal, Lisa and Susan Blake Rowland. 1986. *Academic Reading and Study Skills for International Students.* Englewood Cliffs, NJ: Prentice-Hall. See Chapter 1 on word elements.

Thought Questions

1. Explain why using a dictionary to look up every new word is not a good idea

2. Get is an example of an informal word which has many formal synonyms, each one with a different meaning. Using a dictionary, find five formal synonyms.

3. Every profession has its own set of technical vocabulary. Explain why this is advantageous to those within a particular profession and disadvantageous to those outside of it. Use an example if possible.

4. Various words with similar meanings are used in different fields (Section 6.2). An example of two verbs is order and command. In what profession would each word be used?

5. From the field of computer science, try to find the meaning and origin of the following two technical words: debug and input.

6. A Scottish scientist named James Hutton formulated a theory to explain how the shape of the earth has changed over time. This theory, **uniformitarianism,** assumes that the various forces at work today are the same forces that have always operated. Using your dictionary if necessary, match each word element to its meaning.

   _____ 1. uni   a. shape

   _____ 2. form   b. theory, doctrine

   _____ 3. arian   c. one

   _____ 4. ism   d. advocate of, believer in

Exercises

Exercise A Select the meaning closest to the meaning of the word in boldfaced print. Then underline the word(s) which helped you guess its meaning. The first one is done for you.

1. No one thought that these simple steps could help <u>revive</u> the country's **moribund** economy.

   (a. nearly dead) b. healthy   c. growing

2. Calcium and magnesium are among the most **abundant** of the elements in the Earth's crust, both ranking in the top ten in terms of mass.

   a. visible   b. plentiful   c. heaviest

3. In 1934, tons of dust were picked up by strong winds from large parts of the southwestern United States and carried east. **Prodigious** amounts were deposited in neighboring states.

   a. condensed   b. dirty   c. great

4. Fresh vegetables and other kinds of **perishable** goods present a special shipping problem for manufacturers. Because canned goods have a longer life, they are favored by manufacturers.

   a. heavy   b. capable of spoiling

   c. inexpensive

5. The travelers experienced a feeling of **nostalgia** when they spoke about how they missed their families.

   a. homesickness b. pride c. friendship

6. Some jobs **foster** personal growth, while others may retard it.

   a. decrease   b. promote   c. require

7. The absence of normal social contact during childhood often has a dramatic effect on later social behavior. These effects have been observed in laboratory monkeys reared apart from other monkeys.

   a. raised   b. studied   c. put behind

8. A number of **carcinogenic** substances have been found in polluted city air, but there is no direct evidence that these compounds cause cancer in humans at the concentration observed.

   a. concentrated   b. cancer causing

   c. dirty

9. People who hear noises at regular intervals perform as well as subjects working without interruption. Subjects who are exposed to **random** noises make more errors.

   a. constant b. very loud c. unsystematic

10. One of the main **impediments** to economic development is a lack of education and job skills.

    a. conditions b. problems c. obstructions

Exercise B The following words have technical meanings in addition to their everyday meanings. Try to match the definitions with their fields. The first one is done for you.

1. <u>product</u>   mathematics, chemistry

   _____*mathematics*_____   a. result obtained from multiplying

   _____*chemistry*_____   b. substance produced from a reaction

2. <u>noise</u>   physics, computer science

_____ a. irrelevant or meaningless data

_____ b. disturbance that reduces the quality of a signal

3. <u>hot</u>   physics, electronics

_____ a. radioactive

_____ b. charged or energized

4. <u>gap</u>   automotive mechanics, computer science

_____ a. space through which an electric spark can pass

_____ b. absence of information

5. <u>inactive</u>   medicine, chemistry, physics

_____ a. not participating in reactions

_____ b. having no interaction with organisms

_____ c. having little or no radioactivity

6. <u>table</u>   music, architecture, geology

_____ a. layer of horizontal rock

_____ b. underside of stringed instrument

_____ c. raised rectangular panel on a wall

7. <u>focus</u>   medicine, mathematics, geology

_____ a. point of origin of an earthquake

_____ b. region of an infection

_____ c. point used to determine a conic section

8. <u>negative</u>   mathematics, biology, chemistry, physics

_____ a. referring to an ion attracted to a positive electrode

_____ b. a quantity less than zero

_____ c. resistance to a stimulus

_____ d. pertaining to a body with an excess of electrons

9. <u>depression</u>   meteorology, astronomy, psychiatry, economics

_____ a. condition characterized by an inability to concentrate, and feelings of dejection and guilt

_____   b. great decline in business activity characterized by falling prices and unemployment

_____   c. region of low barometric pressure

_____   d. angular distance of celestial body below the horizon

10. <u>critical</u>   medicine, mathematics, chemistry, physics

_____   a. having sufficient mass to start a nuclear chain reaction

_____   b. pertaining to a life-threatening crisis

_____   c. pertaining to rapid change in a property or quality

_____   d. pertaining to a point where a curve has a maximum or minimum

Exercise C Write the meaning of the underlined word in the spaces provided at the left of each sentence. The first one is done for you.

_____*because*_____   **1.** <u>As</u> the earth turns to the east, places east of us always have an earlier time.

_____   **2.** The enemy army attacked the city just <u>as</u> the city leaders were preparing a statement of surrender.

_____   **3.** Absolute necessities <u>as</u> water are priced quite cheaply, but non-essentials like diamonds are quite expensive.

_____   **4.** Beryllium, both lightweight and strong, is used <u>as</u> windows for X-ray tubes.

_____   **5.** Although the battle plans were executed <u>as</u> they always had been, the outcome this time was quite different.

_____   **6.** <u>As</u> old theories are disproven, they are replaced by better ones.

_____   **7.** A year is <u>but</u> a blink of an eye when thought of in terms of eternity.

_____   **8.** Einstein said that everything should be made as simple as possible, <u>but</u> not more so.

_____   **9.** <u>But</u> for a few close friends, Dickinson had little contact with society.

_____   **10.** Human existence on earth is quite fragile, <u>for</u> it requires a delicate balance of food, clothing, and shelter.

_____   **11.** <u>For</u> all its many useful applications, asbestos has now fallen into disfavor because of its link to lung cancer.

_____ 12. Inflation occurs when there are increases in the average level of prices; <u>however</u>, deflation happens when average prices fall.

_____ 13. <u>However</u> the world was fifty years ago, it has changed greatly from a technological viewpoint.

_____ 14. The theory <u>just</u> discussed has many everyday applications.

_____ 15. The world <u>just</u> might be a little bit better off if we all slowed down.

_____ 16. <u>Just</u> the right amount of sulphur was added to the compound.

_____ 17. Macroeconomics <u>just</u> means the study of various forces which affect the economy as a whole.

_____ 18. <u>Now</u> that acid rain is known to cause crop damage and other problems, ways to limit its formation are under study.

_____ 19. Everything was <u>now</u> in place for the start of the launch.

_____ 20. If you haven't done so already, then <u>now</u> is the time to consider the problem.

_____ 21. <u>Once</u> considered to be an activity reserved only for birds, flying is now second nature to many people.

_____ 22. <u>Once</u> the experiment had ended, the results were compiled and analyzed.

_____ 23. The burning of fossil fuels in an electrical plant involves <u>only</u> three steps.

_____ 24. The primary but not the <u>only</u> raw material for the preparation of potassium compounds is potassium chloride.

_____ 25. Full employment is politically and socially desirable, <u>only</u> it is often economically impracticable.

_____ 26. Our need for oxygen becomes a problem for technology <u>only</u> under water or at very high altitudes.

_____ 27. Five <u>or</u> maybe six applications can be found by studying those theories.

_____ 28. People who lacked either pottery <u>or</u> metal containers solved the problem of how to heat water by stone-boiling.

_____ 29. The Law of Inertia <u>or</u> The First Law of Motion was described by Newton.

_____ 30. Economists tend to concentrate on people's demands <u>since</u> it is more difficult to determine their needs.

_____ 31. <u>Since</u> the development of caloric theory, a number of experiments have been conducted which were found to be at odds with it.

_____ **32.** Sodium is an important element of the alkali metals and <u>so</u> is potassium.

_____ **33.** Carbon dioxide in the atmosphere traps heat that would otherwise escape, and <u>so</u> the world has warmed up by half a degree centigrade since 1850.

_____ **34.** The concept of property is a cultural universal; <u>still</u>, specifics vary widely among human societies.

_____ **35.** They waited until everything was <u>still</u> before they turned on their equipment.

_____ **36.** Psychologists in the West <u>still</u> regard many of Freud's theories as valid.

_____ **37.** When separating a metal from its ore, impurities are often introduced. To correct this, the metal <u>then</u> must be refined.

_____ **38.** World War II followed the Depression. Unemployment in the United States <u>then</u> stood at 15%.

_____ **39.** A refrigerator transfers heat from a colder body to a hotter body. A refrigerator, <u>then</u>, is a heat engine running in reverse.

_____ **40.** <u>While</u> oxidation involves a loss of electrons, reduction involves a gain of electrons.

_____ **41.** <u>While</u> the news reports were being aired, a second attack occurred.

_____ **42.** <u>While</u> Galileo laid the foundation for the science of mechanics, it was Newton who developed the laws of motion.

_____ **43.** Capitalism in its pure form has not <u>yet</u> anywhere been put into practice.

_____ **44.** Before leaving this subject, there is <u>yet</u> a third point to consider.

_____ **45.** The temptation to proceed is great, <u>yet</u> we would be wise to be cautious.

Exercise D Match the formal vocabulary on the left with the informal vocabulary on the right.

_____ 1. attempt	a. use	_____ 9. retain	i. give
_____ 2. employ	b. send	_____ 10. acquire	j. build
_____ 3. speculate	c. begin	_____ 11. comprehend	k. watch
_____ 4. transmit	d. let	_____ 12. transform	l. try
_____ 5. initiate	e. make	_____ 13. exhibit	m. change
_____ 6. formulate	f. keep	_____ 14. permit	n. show
_____ 7. administer	g. understand	_____ 15. observe	o. guess
_____ 8. construct	h. get		

Exercise E Answer the questions concerning the metaphoric language used in the sentences below. The first one is done for you.

1. Giving or receiving aid has a "cost" attached to it.

   What words normally come to mind when we hear <u>cost</u>?

   _____ *buying something; money* _____

2. A living organism is a complex "factory."

   In what way is an organism like a <u>factory</u>?

   _____

3. Various components dissolve into the oceans, eventually forming a chemical "<u>soup</u>."

   In what way is an ocean like <u>soup</u>?

   _____

4. Fossils "label" the rocks in which they occur, providing information about the past.

   What instrument is normally used for <u>labeling</u>?

   _____

5. U.S. dimes and quarters are "sandwiches" of cupronickel around copper.

   How are these coins like <u>sandwiches</u>?

   _____

6. When imports threaten the survival of an industry, the marketplace is signaling that the industry is relatively inefficient and may be "senile."

   <u>Senility</u> is normally associated with what word?

   _____

7. It is not usually necessary to understand computer programming in order to "talk" to a machine.

   <u>Talking</u> is an activity normally associated with what?

   _____

8. Reclamation is an effort to restore land to its original contour and re-establish vegetation to "anchor" the soil.

   What is usually <u>anchored</u> to what?

   _____

9. Carbon monoxide competes with oxygen for the molecule that carries oxygen to the cells. The more carbon monoxide present, the more hemoglobin is "tied up" and the less oxygen can reach the cells.

   What object is suggested by the verb <u>to tie up</u>?

   _____

10. Biologists for many years assumed that the external surface of cells consisted of a cell membrane, although it was not visible even under powerful microscopes. There was no proof that red-celled "ghosts" existed until recently.

    In what way is a <u>ghost</u> like a cell membrane?

    _____

11. The transformation of China from "sleeping giant" into industrial powerhouse took place in a relatively short time.

    Why was China said to be <u>sleeping</u>? In what two ways is it a <u>giant</u>?

    _____

12. When uranium decays, a radioactive gas known as radon is produced. This "daughter" of uranium is dispersed in the air.

    In what way is radon like a <u>daughter</u>?

    _____

13. Consumers make production decisions by buying or not buying certain goods. They "vote" in the marketplace.

    What do people normally choose when they <u>vote</u>?

    _____

14. Sunspots are first seen as "pores" somewhat over 1,500 kms. in diameter.

    Where are <u>pores</u> usually located? Describe them.

    _____

15. Owing to the lack of friction, upper-air winds travel at higher speeds than surface winds. These "rivers" of air move between 75 and 150 mph in a west-to-east direction.

    In what way is the wind like a <u>river</u>?

    _____

Exercise F Describe the picture which comes to mind when you read the underlined words in the sentences below. The first one is done for you.

1. In 1979, a mishap at Three-Mile Island caused nuclear safety to come <u>bubbling up</u> to the top of the world's concerns.

   _____ *boiling water* _____

2. Attempts to <u>checkmate</u> inflation sometimes can drive up the rate of unemployment.

   _____

3. When economies <u>blossom</u>, governments usually receive more money in taxes.

   _____

4. The <u>roots</u> of this idea can be traced back to Aristotle.

   _____

5. All living things depend on each other for survival, and humans are part of the <u>web</u> of life.

   _____

6. The invention of the computer opened a new <u>chapter</u> in the history of technology.

   _____

7. Sales of compact automobiles <u>took off</u> in the mid-1970's owing to the high cost of fuel.

   _____

8. Various types of proteins exist which <u>play</u> an important <u>role</u> in the chemical activities of cells.

   _____

9. The desired effect of a <u>quarantine</u> imposed on one country by another (or others) is political and economic isolation.

   _____

10. When germs <u>invade</u> the body, white blood cells rush to the site of the infection to destroy them.

    _____

Exercise G Fill in the blanks with the appropriate word elements. The first one is partly done for you.

1. biology   = life + study
   geo _logy_   = earth + study
   _____graphy = earth + writing
   _____ = life + writing

2. bilateral   = two + sides
   multi_____ = many + sides
   _____lingual = many + languages
   _____ = two + languages

3. hydrometer   = water + measure
   thermo_____   = heat + measure
   _____tropism = heat + growth
   _____ = water + growth

4. television   = far + see
   _____phone = far + sound
   micro_____ = small + sound
   _____scope = small + see

CHAPTER 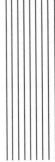 **7**

Style

Study Objectives

By the end of this chapter, you should be able to:

- recognize ways that authors achieve variety in their writing;
- identify ways that authors can omit and abbreviate words.

In this chapter, you will study two elements of style widely found in textbooks: variety and brevity. You will see how authors avoid (1) using lengthy words repeatedly, and (2) using more words than are necessary.

7.1 Synonyms and Superordinates

Authors frequently use **synonyms** to add variety and interest to their writing. A synonym is a word which is similar in meaning to another one. For example, <u>automobile</u> is synonymous with <u>car</u>. Examine the use of synonyms for <u>cities</u> in the following passage.

> The economic advantages of cities often make them worthwhile places for people to live in. In addition, metropolises are stimulating and can provide a wider range of experiences than rural or suburban settings. All in all, urban centers provide enriching atmospheres.

cities = _____ = _____

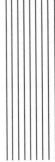

107

Synonyms are related to superordinates. A superordinate is a word which names a larger category to which another word belongs. Refer to Table 6.1 if necessary to answer the following:

super = _____

Using the example of a car, find its superordinate in the following diagram. Can you complete the diagram?

vehicle

| |

_____ | _____

| | | | |

car   truck   train   _____   _____

The superordinate for "car" is _____

While synonyms are often interchangeable, superordinates are not. If you understand the difference between them, you should be able to complete the following sentences using <u>automobiles</u>, <u>cars</u>, and <u>vehicles</u>.

All automobiles are cars, and all

cars are _____.

All automobiles are vehicles, but not all

_____ are _____.

The following two passages, taken from physics and business, contain superordinates. Read them and complete the exercises that follow them.

A hungry bear weighing 160 lbs. walks out on a beam to eat some honey at the end. The beam is uniform, weighs 50 lbs, and is 20 ft. long; the food weighs 5 lbs. When the animal is 3 ft. from the end, the beam breaks.

superordinate

bear: _____

honey: _____

In 1940, farmers constituted nearly 25% of the work force in the United States. By 1980, the percentage of these workers had decreased to slightly under 5%. Agriculture may employ far fewer people today than forty years ago, but this industry provides much more food than ever before.

superordinate

farmers: _____

agriculture: _____

7.2 Substitution

In order to avoid needless repetition of one or more words, authors will often replace them with a shorter word. An example of this can be found in the sentence you have just read.

<u>them</u> = _____

Substitution efficiently reduces the length of a sentence. Table 7.1 lists common substitutes and examples of their use. In the first example, both the substitute and the words it refers to are underlined. You do the underlining for the other examples.

TABLE 7.1: Common Word Substitutes

Noun Substitutes	I, we, you, they he, she, it,	The <u>languages of Africa</u> number as many as one thousand. <u>They</u> are mostly of the Niger-Congo family.
	me, us, you, them him, her, it, one	The 1972 food crop was a poor one throughout the world.
	all, most, many some, few, none	Australia, Britain, Canada, Holland, Sweden and Saudi Arabia provide free health care for their nationals. All are among the world's richer nations.
	this, that these, those	Certain organisms carry disease. These include viruses, bacteria, worms, and insects.
	each, both either, neither	Gold and silver are precious metals. Both have industrial uses.

Noun Substitutes	the former the latter ("Former" refers to the first item, while "latter" refers to the second of the two)	Petroleum-based products provide most of our energy needs. However, the use of solar power has been increasing significantly. The former are in limited supply, but the supply of the latter is nearly infinite.
Time Substitutes	then at that time	The Great Wall of China was built during the Han Dynasty (202 B.C. to A.D. 220). The Great Wall was needed to establish boundaries and provide a system of national defense at that time.
Place Substitutes	here, there	Japan has a very limited base of natural resources. Out of necessity, raw materials are shipped there from all over the world.
Process Substitutes	in this/that way like this/that	When we eat food, we also ingest harmful organisms. Sickness and disease often originate in this way.

A substitution usually refers to something that has already been mentioned in a reading. <u>It</u> might be in the same sentence or in a previous sentence.

<u>It</u> refers to _____, which is found in...

    a. the same sentence.

    b. a previous sentence.

The following passage, taken from astronomy, contains several substitutions.

Several hundred years ago, Galileo and then Newton looked at motion and concluded that there was a more productive way to view <u>it</u>. The <u>former</u> decided that the natural state of matter is to remain in motion once <u>it</u> is set in motion.

    it = _____

  former = _____

    it = _____

Occasionally, substitutions refer to something that has not yet been identified in the reading. When this happens, the substitution nearly always refers to something in the same sentence.

When <u>they</u> lose electrons, the atoms become positively charged ions.

they = _____

Since <u>it</u> was first introduced in the 1950's, the Results Management school has grown in popularity within the business world.

it = _____

Examine the many substitutions in the following paragraph.

One characteristic of written English is that <u>it</u> economizes on words. <u>This</u> is particularly true of the kind of writing found in textbooks. In <u>this</u> chapter, we examine two ways that writers commonly do <u>that</u>. The first <u>one</u> is called **substitution** and the second is called ellipsis. Substitution and **ellipsis** often cause confusion to students who are unprepared to meet <u>them</u> in <u>their</u> reading.

it = _____

this = _____

this = _____

that = _____

one = _____

them = _____

their = _____

It probably was not too difficult to locate the words these substitutions refer to. A textbook reading can become difficult when: (1) a substitution is far from the word it refers to; (2) there are many substitutions. Consider the following examples.

As <u>it</u> hits an object, the wind sweeps over and around <u>it</u>, leaving a pocket of slower-moving air immediately behind the object along with a similar but smaller pocket in front of <u>it</u>. In these pockets, sand particles drop. Soon, a sand dune forms.

it = _____

it = _____

it = _____

Extending from 12 to 30 degrees N latitude, the Red Sea lies in a highly arid region of the world. The maximum width of the sea is slightly more than 300 km, occurring in the southern end between Ethiopia and Yemen. To the north just below the split that forms the Gulf of Suez and the Gulf of Aqaba, it narrows to approximately 145 km.

the sea = _____

it = _____

7.3 Ellipsis

Another way that authors avoid repetition is by omitting unneeded words. This process is called **ellipsis**. You will find that this process is at work in most sentences in your textbooks. Ellipsis is used in order to minimize the number of words in a reading. Like substitution, some occurrences of ellipsis are quite easy to see. Other occurrences of ellipsis, however, are not easy to see.

There are no instances of ellipsis in the paragraph you have just read. The total number of words used was 66. Compare the length of that paragraph with the next one.

Another way (that) authors avoid repetition is by omitting unneeded words. This (process) is called ellipsis. Ellipsis is used (in order) to minimize the number of words in a reading. You will find (that) this (process is) at work in most sentences in your textbooks. Like substitution, some occurrences (of ellipsis) are quite easy to see. Other occurrences (of ellipsis), however, are not (easy to see).

By omitting the words in parentheses, the total number of words decreases.

number of words in original: 66

number of words in parentheses: – _____

total: _____

Economy of words is what ellipsis is all about. Further examples of ellipsis can be found in Table 7.2. In this table, you will see that the first example of each group comes with the omitted word(s) in parentheses. You will need to complete the other examples.

TABLE 7.2: Examples of Ellipsis

Verbs	The continental shelf has not always been submerged, but undoubtedly will be (<u>submerged</u>) for many more years.
	Imports must decrease and the money supply (_____) increase before the economy improves.
Subjects	Mendeleev prepared a study of the arrangement of elements and then (____) published his findings.
	Newton developed classical mechanics as a systematic theory and (_____) was one of the first to use calculus as a mathematical tool.
Dependent Clauses	If (<u>paper is</u>) recycled, paper can remain an abundant source of raw materials.
	Although (_____) very scarce, food could be found to sustain the population.
	When (_____) balanced, the equation must obey the law of conservation of mass.
	(_____) Like it or (_____) not (_____), the results of the study were not seen as proof of the theory.
Adjective Clauses	No one (<u>who is</u>) intelligent can be fooled by those arguments.
	Debris (_____) washed down slopes will form deposits at the bottom.
	Wind (_____) blowing from left to right stripped the field.
	Scientists subscribing (=<u>who subscribed</u>) to the notion that matter cannot forever be divided were proven correct.
	An economy having (=_____) a responsible system of banks will maintain the confidence of the public.

Possessive Forms	His experiments verified his colleague's (<u>experiments</u>).
	Dalton's (_____) is a theory of atoms that is still adhered to.
General Nouns	The starving (= <u>people who are starving</u>) can count on at least some relief in the near future.
	The worried (=_____) may find some hope in the findings of this study.
	The French (=_____) have recently instituted a number of social reforms.
	The medical profession is committed to helping the sick (=_____).

7.4 Abbreviations

An abbreviation is a shortened form of a word used in order to avoid repetition of long expressions. Abbreviations can be of two sorts. One type consists of only enough letters of a word for readers to recognize it. Examples of this type can be found in Table 7.3. The second type of abbreviation consists of the first letter of each major word in an expression. Examples of this type can be found in Table 7.4.

TABLE 7.3: Type I Abbreviations

Description	Abbreviation	Full Form
Beginning Letters Retained	diag. diam. esp. gal.	diagram, diagonal diameter especially gallon
First and Last Letters Retained	dept. int'l. kt. qty.	department international karat quantity

TABLE 7.4: Type II Abbreviations

Description	Abbreviation	Full Form
First Letter of Each Major Word Retained	b.p.	boiling point
	Btu	British thermal unit
	p.s.i.	pounds per square inch
	r.m.s.	root mean square
	GPA	grade point average
	IMF	International Monetary Fund
	VAT	value added tax

An author will usually introduce an expression in full before abbreviating it. The abbreviation will be enclosed in parentheses immediately following the full form. Each time after that, the abbreviation will be used without the parentheses. Examine the following passage.

> The Gross National Product (GNP) is the total value of the goods and services produced in a country during one year. GNP is a useful tool for determining the rate at which an economy is expanding or contracting.

A small number of abbreviations come from Latin expressions. These are listed in Table 7.5 on the following page, with their meanings in English and their full forms in Latin. The full forms in Latin are seldom used in English.

TABLE 7.5: Abbreviations Derived from Latin

Abbreviation	Full Latin Form Followed by English Meaning	Example
c. or ca.	circa approximately	Antonio Lopez de Santa Anna, born c. 1797 and died 1876, was a political and military leader from Mexico.
e.g.	exempli gratia for example	Natural boundaries often form political boundaries (e.g., the Pyrenees between Spain and France).
et al.	et alii and others	Pierson et al. studied the spread of malaria.
etc.	et cetera and so on	Perishible goods, such as fruit, vegetables, etc., are those which have a very short life.
i.e.	id est that is	Matter can exist in three states, i.e., solid, liquid, and gas.

Because certain abbreviations are so well known, authors assume that you are already familiar with them. Consequently, their full forms will not be given. If you need to know the meaning of an unfamiliar abbreviation, your dictionary will help. Some dictionaries list abbreviations along with all the other entries. Other dictionaries list them in a special section in an appendix. Many of the most frequently-used abbreviations that you can expect to meet in textbooks are listed in Appendix A.

7.5 Symbols and Punctuation

A **symbol** is a special sign that represents a word or a concept. Every academic field has its own special set of symbols which you will need to learn. There are, however, certain symbols that are commonly found in almost all textbooks. Try matching some of these below.

_____	1. #	a. and
_____	2. @	b. at
_____	3. %	c. dollar(s)
_____	4. $	d. number
_____	5. &	e. per cent

Various forms of punctuation marks are really symbols because they, too, represent words or concepts. Many of the most common of these forms are identified in Table 7.6.

TABLE 7.6: Punctuation as Symbols

Punctuation Mark	Use or Meaning	Example
Slash /	or	s/he (=she or he), and/or
	per/every	45 km/hr.
	and	1987/88
Dash -	through	pages 24-8 the years 1650-1690
	to	the New York-Paris flight
Parentheses ( )	dates lived	Marie and Pierre Curie (1867-1934, 1859-1906) devoted their lives to scientific research.
	optional plurals	The effect(s) of solar power... (= the effect or the effects of solar power...)
	synonyms	The owner of a firm is responsible for its liabilities (debts).
	abbreviations	Uses for Artificial Intelligence (AI) have been found in nearly every field.
	examples	Various means of public transporta-tion (bus, train, plane) will be utilized.

	identifiers	Matter exists in three states (solid, liquid, gas). Companies like Chrysler (cars), Columbia House (records) and Pepsico (soft drinks) export their products. When the nitrogen oxide pollution problem disappears, another one (hydrocarbon emission) takes its place.
	citations	The long-term effects of high noise levels on people have been the subject of various studies (Scheller, 1981; Prince and Lane, 1985). = a study published in 1981 which was written by David Scheller, and another one which was published in 1985 which was written by Eugene Prince and Kenneth Lane.
Quotation Marks " "	direct speech	Descartes said, "I think, therefore I am."
	analogy	A telescope is an astronomer's "eye."
	loose or inexact meaning	For twenty years, some factories have been "temporarily" storing toxic wastes. The world's first oil-producing well was started up by "Colonel" E.L. Drake in Titusville, Pennsylvania.

7.6 Footnotes and Asterisks

You will notice that some sentences in your readings end with either a raised number or a star-shaped figure. The number is called a **superscript** number (super = above, script = writing) and the figure is called an **asterisk** (aster = star). These symbols refer you elsewhere for additional information.

The asterisk or superscript number is repeated at the beginning of the information that it refers to. When this information is at the bottom of the same page, it is called **a footnote**. When it is at the end of the chapter or book, it is called an **endnote**. A footnote* or endnote adds useful information that does not easily fit into a reading or that is considered less important. In this paragraph, which symbol was used to send you to the footnote?

_____ asterisk   _____ superscript

Read the following passage and explain why the author has used a footnote instead of putting this information into the passage.

> While performing routine laboratory operations, solutions are commonly diluted. For example, sulphuric acid must be diluted before it can be used.[1] The process of dilution simply involves spreading a certain amount of solute throughout a larger volume of solution.

reason for
use of footnote: _____

The numbering system for footnotes and endnotes will begin anew in each chapter. The first footnote in the next chapter will have the number '1'.

Summary

In this chapter, you learned ways that authors try to add variety to their writing and achieve conciseness in it. They do this by substituting one word for another, by using abbreviations, symbols, and certain forms of punctuation, and by dropping unnecessary words.

Key Vocabulary

abbreviation	ellipsis	footnote	substitution	superscript	synonym
asterisk	endnote	number	superordinate	symbol	

Recommended Reading

Leech, Geoffrey and Jan Svartvik. 1985. *A Communicative Grammar of English*. Essex, England: Longman Group. See Part 3, Section D on reference and ellipsis.

---

* Congratulations. You found the footnote.

[1] Never add water to a concentrated acid. Always add the acid to the solvent.

Thought Questions

1. In Section 7.1 we saw that synonyms are words with "roughly" the same meaning. If we wanted to use a word which means "to look at for an extended time," we could choose from among the following: gaze, stare, gape, and glare. Although these words are roughly synonymous, they cannot be used interchangeably. Find out how they differ.

2. Supply several examples for each of the following superordinates: creature, object, emotion, furniture, game, appliance.

3. Make a list of common abbreviations, dividing them into Types I and II. Group them according to form.

4. Nearly all abbreviations retain some letters of the full word, making them easily identifiable. One exception is the abbreviation for pound, a unit of weight. How is it abbreviated? Try to find out why.

5. With the help of a dictionary, find the symbols for the following words: comet (astronomy), male (biology), gold (chemistry), therefore (mathematics and logic), poison (medicine), beta ray (physics), hurricane (meteorology).

Exercises

Exercise A Find any synonymous nouns or superordinates in the passages below and write them in the spaces provided. The first one is done for you.

1. The oscilloscope is used to make electrical measurements. The principal component of this instrument is the cathode ray tube.

   oscilloscope = _instrument_

2. An alternating current generator converts mechanical energy into electrical energy. This device operates on the principle of electromagnetic induction.

   _____ = _____

3. There are two explanations of how Polynesians came to live on the islands of the South Pacific. The first holds that voyages were deliberate; the alternative view is that settling was accidental, and that the travelers drifted off course.

   _____ = _____

4. Any one of the many parts of an airplane is incapable of producing flight. Together, they form a flying machine.

   _____ = _____

5. In 1642, Pascal invented an automatic contraption that could add or substract. Unfortunately, the gadget never became popular because the clerks of his day saw it as a potential job threat. It was not until some years later that Leibniz added the power of multiplication and division. Although mechanical contrivances such as these really were no more than calculators, their inventions are seen as milestones in the history of the development of the modern computer.

   _____ = _____ = _____

6. Eisenhower could hardly have been less like Churchill. The American was quiet and felt uncomfortable with power. The Englishman was eloquent and assumed authority quite naturally.

_____ = _____

_____ = _____

7. Automobiles powered by gasoline engines are really quite inefficient machines. Even under ideal conditions, only a small percentage of the available energy in the fuel is used to power these vehicles.

_____ = _____ = _____

8. Pottery-making appeared in the Near East a little under 8,000 years ago, and its techniques spread rapidly. This craft is found anywhere farming is found as well as among food-collecting peoples.

_____ = _____

9. When a gas is introduced into a container, the molecules move freely within it and occupy the entire volume. The volume of a gas, therefore, is the same as the vessel in which it is held.

_____ = _____

10. The most pressing needs of developing nations are huge injections of capital, introduction of new technology, and substantial education and job training programs. Developed countries are in a good position to provide these.

_____ = _____

Exercise B   Write the full forms for the underlined substitutions.

1. While the newborn's sense of smell is relatively weak immediately after birth, it seems to improve within the first few days.

    it = _____

2. The eye sends signals to the brain. These then are used to tell the color of the light it sees.

    these = _____

    it = _____

3. Melting and boiling points are frequently referred to as constants, meaning that they do not change. This is not entirely accurate because we know that the boiling point of water does change with altitude.

    they = _____

    this = _____

4. Pollution can occur anywhere, but in low population density areas at such low rates that it does not pose the same kind of environmental threat that it does in urban areas.

    it = _____

    it = _____

5. Konrad Zuse built a simple computer that could manage a rather wide variety of tasks. Its descendants were used in World War II to calculate wing designs for the German aircraft industry. Some found other military uses.

    its = _____

    some = _____

6. Psychologists trained a chimpanzee named Washoe to use Standard American Sign Language, a language used by deaf people. Communication was made by using gestures only. By the time she was five years old, Washoe's vocabulary consisted of 130 signs. More importantly, she seemed able to put them together in creative ways.

she = _____

them = _____

7. Eyes are subject to several diseases. One of <u>them</u>, occurring largely in old age, is characterized by the formation of cataracts. <u>These</u> are opaque growths over the lens, and the only known remedy is surgery.

them = _____

these = _____

8. Buildings protect people from the surrounding weather. To do <u>this</u>, <u>they</u> must be designed to respond to changing weather conditions as well as to the comfort requirements of the user.

this = _____

they = _____

9. Gaspard Monge is known as the "Father of Modern Descriptive Geometry." During his

life, <u>he</u> was assigned to Napoleon when <u>he</u> was general and <u>he</u> served <u>him</u> as a scientific and technical aide.

he = _____

he = _____

he = _____

him = _____

10. In the 1600s, scientists re-examined the idea that "nature abhors a vacuum." Until <u>then</u>, everyone from Aristotle to Descartes had accepted <u>it</u> uncritically. Indeed, many theories of the <u>former</u> were based on this proposition.

then = _____

it = _____

former = _____

Exercise C Rewrite the following sentences to include the words in parentheses found after each sentence. The first one is done for you.

1. Different people have different needs, and these are often culturally-conditioned. (needs) (needs)

   Different people have different needs and these needs are often culturally conditioned needs.

2. Believe it or not, there is sufficient evidence to prove the thesis. (whether you) (whether you do) (believe it)

   _____

   _____

   _____

   _____

3. The best writers can do is hope their work is widely read and understood. (thing that) (that)

   _____

   _____

   _____

   _____

4. Humans die if kept awake for long periods of time. (they are)

   _____

   _____

   _____

   _____

5. The average office worker in the U.S. rises at seven o'clock and at eight-thirty steps into the car for the drive to work. (o'clock) (the average office worker in the U.S.)

_____

_____

_____

_____

6. Although not distinguished by any one characteristic, the fungal groups have much in common. (the fungal groups) (are)

_____

_____

_____

7. The ordinary well is simply a hole dug or drilled in an area where ground water is unconfirmed. (that is) (a hole that is)

_____

_____

_____

8. There are three stages which may be but do not have to be followed in the development of writing. (followed) (which)

_____

_____

_____

_____

9. All varieties of cheese are produced as a result of bacterial action, and many as a result of fungal action as well. (varieties of cheese are produced)

_____

_____

_____

_____

10. Radioactive waste includes any materials extracted and discarded during either the manufacture or the use of radioactive materials, and covers a number of different conditions. (that are) (that are) (of radioactive materials) (during) (this)

_____

_____

_____

_____

Exercise D The letters in parentheses show places where words have been omitted through the use of ellipsis. Write the omitted words in the corresponding blanks. The first one is done for you.

1. Plants do not have the sophisticated protective mechanisms (a) possessed by animals. They are, however, capable of repelling certain infections. Land plants are successful in living a long life in part because of their rigid structure which keeps them standing upright. When (b) upright, they are protected by their outer layers, which are thick and water-repellent.

a _that are_   b. _land plants are_

2. Lavoisier defined elements as substances which cannot be further simplified. In a fundamental sense, this definition has survived to this day but (a) needs some modification in the light of certain recent technological developments. With the invention of the particle accelerator and (b) atom smasher, it has become possible to break elements down. Consequently, chemists now define elements as substances (c) unable to be broken down by chemical means.

a. _____ c. _____

b. _____

3. A building developer is an individual or (a) legal entity such as a partnership or (b) corporation (c) engaged in the business of creating buildings for investment purposes. Developers may be involved in building or renovating small houses or (d) building industrial complexes. Except for certain public buildings such as police stations, libraries, schools, or hospitals, most of our environment is shaped by these individuals and organizations.

a. _____ c. _____

b. _____ d. _____

4. In the 1340s, the Black Death first appeared in Italy and (a) spread throughout Europe during the following two decades. Because no accurate mortality records were kept, we can only estimate the number of deaths. Certainly, some towns lost as many as 40% of their inhabitants. Although the worst (b) was over by 1360, repeated (c) but less severe outbreaks occurred for the next fifty years. These (d) kept the population (e) from returning to its pre-plague numbers.

a. _____ d. _____

b. _____ e. _____

c. _____

5. The field of biology is extraordinarily large. Thus, as much out of convenience as (a) necessity, biology is divided into subdisciplines (b) divided in turn into various specialized areas of study. For our purposes, we shall identify two broad disciplines (c) linked with one another: the first (d) includes those areas (e) determined by the organisms (f) examined; the second (g) comprises areas (h) covered by the approach (i) taken to the subject matter.

a. _____ f. _____

b. _____ g. _____

c. _____ h. _____

d. _____ i. _____

e. _____

Exercise E Explain in the spaces provided what the symbols in the underlined expressions stand for or represent. The first two are done for you.

_____*to*_____ 1. The <u>Tokyo-Seattle</u> route is frequently used for Pacific crossings.

_____*synonym*_____ 2. Energy can take on various forms, including mechanical, electromagnetic, chemical, thermal <u>(heat)</u>, and nuclear energy.

_____ 3. In the United States, prices fell by an average of one third in the years <u>1929-1933</u>.

_____ 4. A tropical storm has wind speeds of 63-118 <u>km/hr</u>.

_____ 5. The <u>price(s)</u> can be established after the quotas are set.

_____ 6. For a spacecraft to leave the Earth, an initial velocity of about <u>7 m/sec</u>. must be reached at an altitude of several hundred miles.

_____ 7. <u>Pages 52-8</u> discuss the applications of this theory.

_____ **8.** Sir Walter Raleigh <u>(1552?-1618)</u> was an English navigator and writer.

_____ **9.** The demand for a given product depends on the marginal benefit <u>(utility)</u> received from consuming it.

_____ **10.** Alvin Toffler authored *Future Shock* <u>(1970)</u>, a book which examined difficulties in adapting to the fast pace of the future.

_____ **11.** The <u>linguistic/sociological</u> importance of the study is not yet known.

_____ **12.** Dick Rutan <u>(1938-)</u> and Jeana Yeager <u>(1952-)</u> set a record in 1986 by flying around the world without refueling.

_____ **13.** One generally accepted practice in inventory control is called first-in, first-out <u>(FIFO)</u>.

_____ **14.** <u>S/he</u> will be chosen on the basis of past performance and future expectations.

_____ **15.** The conference was chaired by Bello <u>(U.S.A.)</u> and Hadjaj-Aoul <u>(Algeria)</u>.

Exercise F Write the appropriate Latin abbreviations in the spaces in the passage. Then write their full forms in English in the spaces provided at the end of the passage. The first one is done for you.

One team of researchers (Riley ___*et al*___) has traced the first observations of electric and magnetic phenomena to Greece (_____ 800). Many of these observations were based upon everyday occurrences. When amber is rubbed, for instance, it becomes electrified and attracts straw, feathers, _____ . Knowledge of magnetic forces came by observing that magnetite is attracted to iron. In fact, the word electric comes from a Greek word (_____ , elektron) and magnetic comes from Magnesia, the city in Asia Minor where magnetite was found. Throughout the ages, many scientists and inventors (_____ , Coulomb, Oersted, Faraday, Maxwell, Hertz, Marconi) have continued the study of electromagnetism.

1. _____*and others*_____   **4.** _____

2. _____   **5.** _____

3. _____

CHAPTER 8

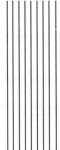

Integrative Reading

Study Objectives

By the end of this chapter, you should be able to:

- recognize the importance of integrating information both within and across topics.

8.1 Integrating Information

As you read through a textbook, you acquire knowledge. Almost always, this new knowledge is in some way related to knowledge that you already possess. Often, it is also related to knowledge you are acquiring from textbooks in other classes that you are taking. As you study, your task is to combine this knowledge with what you already know and what you are learning in your other classes. This process of putting together information from several sources is called **integration**.

Consider, for example, what may be learned by integrating knowledge from the following sources. A physics book may discuss the nucleus of the uranium atom and the way in which energy is released in nuclear fission. A history book may discuss how the atom bomb, which obtains its energy from nuclear fission, influenced the outcome of World War II. A textbook from ecology may provide information on the environmental damage caused by an atomic explosion. Textbooks in the fields of psychology, anthropology, and genetics may add related information. Finally, you probably have previous knowledge about atomic bombs or other uses of atomic power. By integrating all your various sources of information — both old and new — you gain a rounded picture of a subject that you cannot acquire from one source alone.

The integration of newly-acquired knowledge is, of course, not limited to the years you are in school or university. This process continues all your life. In this chapter, however, you will see how information from various textbooks can be integrated.

8.2 Integrating Within Topics

Every topic has various sides to it. When you study one textbook, one side of that topic will be emphasized. A textbook from a different subject may present information emphasizing a different side of the same topic. In this section, you will have opportunities to integrate these sides into a whole. The two passages below, taken from history and medical science, address the topic of lead poisoning. Each passage is followed by comprehension questions requiring an answer of true or false.

Historians have long speculated as to the causes leading to the decline and fall of the Roman Empire. One of the most interesting theories holds that lead poisoning contributed to the downfall of Rome. The water pipes used by the Romans were made of lead. In fact, the English word for plumbing comes from the ancient Latin word for lead, "plumbum." Pipes made of lead contaminate the drinking water. Consumption of that water over a long period may result in brain damage, anemia, and a condition marked by restlessness and even violent behavior. Although lead poisoning in itself was probably not sufficient to cause a collapse of this once-mighty civilization, it could have been a contributing factor.

_____ 1. The passage establishes that lead is a substance which was identified long ago.

_____ 2. The passage establishes that lead can be used to transport liquids.

_____ 3. The passage establishes that lead is harmful when it is consumed.

_____ 4. The passage establishes that lead must be consumed in order to be harmful.

_____ **5.** The passage establishes that the effects of lead poisoning are reversible if people stop consuming lead-contaminated substances.

_____ **6.** The passage implies that the people of Rome were unaware of the dangers of lead poisoning.

_____ **7.** The passage implies that most Romans drank water transported in pipes made of lead.

_____ **8.** The passage implies that the more lead-contaminated water people drank, the sicker they became.

_____ **9.** The passage implies that crimes probably increased as a result of extensive lead poisoning.

_____ **10.** The passage implies that lead poisoning was the principal reason leading to the collapse of the Roman Empire.

> Metals such as mercury, lead, cadmium, chromium, and thallium are all poisonous when taken internally in sufficient quantities. Mercury is particularly dangerous because the body has no easy means of ridding itself of this element. However, because people have greater occasion to come into contact with lead than with most other poisonous metals, lead poisoning leads the list of toxic illnesses.

> Lead is present in foods, water supplies, and even the air. Fortunately, the body is able is eliminate approximately two milligrams per day through the kidneys and intestinal tract. When the level of lead exceeds this limit, the body must store it in tissues and bone.

_____ **11.** The passage establishes that lead must be consumed in significant amounts to be considered poisonous.

_____ **12.** The passage establishes that lead poisoning causes people to become sicker than mercury poisoning does.

_____ **13.** The passage establishes that more people are affected by mercury poisoning than by lead poisoning.

_____ **14.** The passage establishes what the long-term effects of lead poisoning are.

_____ **15.** The passage establishes how lead is removed from the body.

_____ **16.** The passage implies that the consumption of lead in small quantities probably causes no or few noticeable effects.

_____ **17.** The passage implies that pipes are still the primary source of lead poisoning.

_____ **18.** The passage implies that lead can enter our bodies when we breathe.

_____ **19.** The passage implies that amounts of lead under two milligrams a day are probably considered to be acceptable.

_____ **20.** The passage implies that the storage of lead in tissues and bone is undesirable.

The preceding two passages presented information which helped you to increase your understanding of lead poisoning. By integrating this information, you should have been able to establish the following facts:

1. The history of lead poisoning is a long one.
2. Lead poisoning continues to be a problem.
3. When taken into the body over long periods of time and in sufficient quantities, the effects of lead poisoning are extremely harmful.

A further step is integrating these facts with information you already know about lead poisoning and information you can acquire from newspapers, magazines, radio, and television, or from talking with others. Consider such questions as the following:

1. What segment or part of the population is most likely to be poisoned by lead today?

2. In what ways has the understanding of lead poisoning affected the automobile industry? The petroleum industry? The paint industry? The plumbing industry?

3. How has an understanding of the dangers of lead poisoning affected people who sell or rent houses or apartments?

8.3 Integrating Across Topics

In this section, you will see that a topic from one textbook can be linked to a different topic in a textbook from a different field. The following four passages, taken from human anatomy, molecular biology, pathology, and the physiology of exercise, all provide different pieces of a puzzle. As you read through them, try to see the relationship between them. Each passage is followed by comprehension questions to be answered with <u>true</u> or <u>false</u>.

Macrophages

The human body contains approximately three trillion cells. One out of every hundred functions to protect the other cells from foreign invaders. These soldier cells are the body's white blood cells, which are manufactured in the bone marrow.

One type of white blood cell is called a **macrophage**. These cells help fight off any enemy, but more importantly, they are responsible for sounding the general alarm that brings other white cells to the battlefront.

_____ 1. The passage establishes that a majority of the body's cells aid in fighting any foreign invaders.

_____ 2. The passage establishes that one of every one hundred of the body's cells is a white blood cell.

_____ 3. The passage establishes the origin of white blood cells.

_____ 4. The passage implies that there is only one type of white blood cell.

_____ 5. The passage implies that macrophages are unable to defeat foreign invaders alone.

Stress

When people show signs of nervousness and distress owing to mental strain or pressure, they are said to be experiencing **stress**. The feelings associated with stress will last as long as the situation causing stress does, and sometimes even longer. For example, students may feel stress before and during an exam, but these feelings will probably lessen when the exam is finished. Soldiers fighting a war will quite naturally feel stress, which may develop into a condition known as "battle fatigue." People working in high pressure jobs, such as police officers, air traffic controllers, or company executives, will feel the effects of stress over a long period of time. Eventually, this condition may develop into what is known as "burnout," and these people will no longer be able to function effectively in their jobs.

_____ **6.** The passage establishes that stress may last only a short time or may continue indefinitely.

_____ **7.** The passage establishes that battle fatigue is a mild form of stress.

_____ **8.** The passage implies that there are many ways people can reduce stress.

_____ **9.** The passage implies that people working in stressful jobs might be in poorer health than people who are not.

_____**10.** The passage implies that people suffering from burnout might be able to function effectively if they changed jobs.

Cortisol

When people undergo physical or emotional stress, the body reacts chemically. One of the brain's control centers known as the hypothalamus sends out a signal that eventually reaches the adrenal gland. This gland releases a substance throughout the body called **cortisol** that raises the amount of sugar in the blood. This additional sugar provides fuel to the body, in effect increasing the body's energy level. Cortisol, however, also impedes the effectiveness of macrophages, one of the body's first line of defense against disease.

_____**11.** The passage establishes that the hypothalamus is directly responsible for the release into the body of cortisol.

_____**12.** The passage establishes the location of the adrenal gland.

_____**13.** The passage implies that the brain houses more than one control center.

_____**14.** The passage implies that an increased amount of blood sugar during periods of emotional stress is probably desirable and beneficial.

_____ **15.** The passage implies that the presence of cortisol in the body might lower resistance to disease.

Exercise

Any activity that is aimed at developing the physical condition of the body can be termed **exercise**. Studies have shown that some types of exercise are more helpful than others. In fact, certain forms of exercise can even be counterproductive.

Recommended types of exercise are the so-called endurance exercises: swimming, bicycling, running, sports, and so on. These are exercises that develop the lungs, enabling them to deliver more oxygen to the blood and body tissues. People who are in better physical condition can more readily utilize oxygen, which is needed to combat physical as well as mental stress.

_____ **16.** The passage establishes that exercise has more beneficial effects than not.

_____ **17.** The passage establishes a link between endurance exercises and better health.

_____ **18.** The passage establishes the role that oxygen plays in combating stress.

_____ **19.** The passage implies that some types of exercise are not recommended.

_____ **20.** The passage implies that the better physical condition people are in, the more oxygen they can utilize.

The preceding four passages presented information which aided you in seeing the interconnectedness of stress, disease, and exercise. By integrating information from each, you should have been able to establish the following facts:

1. Endurance exercising helps in reducing stress.

2. Stress prevents the body from fighting off disease effectively.

Again here, you can integrate the facts you learned with information you already know as well as with information from other sources, including your own experiences. Do you know of persons who have become ill as a result of stress? Do you know of anyone who has experienced "burnout"? Do you know any people who are almost never ill, or any people who seem to become ill far more frequently than others? Do the passages you have read help you to understand these people? Why or why not?

You may find when studying a particular problem that textbooks in each field will contain their own explanations about the problem's causes. For example, a biology text may suggest that crime can be traced to genes or heredity. A sociology text may place the blame on the environment or on society. A psychology text may explain that an unhappy childhood causes crime. An economics text may point out that a relationship exists between crime and the general state of business. A meteorology text may inform you that more crimes occur in areas where there is a high number of positive ions in the air than in areas with a low number of positive ions. And so on.

Each textbook will probably contain research results or other data that support its point of view. It is your responsibility to evaluate and integrate the different explanations, using some of the skills you have learned in *Inside Textbooks*. Test each explanation against your own experience as well as against the other explanations. Then decide on an explanation that takes all of these into account.

Summary

In this chapter, you examined the importance of viewing pieces of information as part of a larger whole. You saw how information from one textbook might relate to that in another. This relationship might be within a particular topic or across several topics.

Key Vocabulary

integration

Thought Questions

1. Make a list of the types of textbooks and the topics contained within them that might relate to the subject of energy sources, including oil and coal as well as nuclear, solar, and wind power.

2. Make a list of the kinds of textbooks that might contain the following topics: how to-bacco is grown; how cigarettes are made; what the connection is between smoking and respiratory illnesses; and how cigarette sales are an important source of tax revenue for many countries.

3. Choose a topic of current interest and identify the social, economic, political, and sci-

entific aspects of it. What kinds of textbooks might help you in integrating information about this subject?

4. Go to your library and select a botany book that describes the frankincense tree. From a history book, find out about the frankincense trail (an ancient trade route originating in the Arabian Peninsula). Write a composition that incorporates information from the two sources.

5. Locate an earth science textbook in your school library and read about the destructive effects of earthquakes. From an architecture textbook, read about earthquake-resistant buildings. Write a composition incorporating information from both sources.

Exercises

Exercise A   The following passages come from chemistry, economics, geology, and history. All are about "gold." After each passage are comprehension questions that require an answer of <u>true</u> or <u>false</u>.

Gold (chemical symbol Au from the Latin "aurum") is a naturally occurring substance, and as such, is relatively rare. Gold is extremely soft, which allows it to be easily shaped, but it is also quite heavy. This property, in addition to its beautiful yellow color, makes it highly suitable for use as jewelry and decoration. Because gold is also a very good conductor of electricity and heat, it is used as a plated coating on a wide variety of electrical and mechanical components.

_____ **1.** The passage establishes that naturally occurring substances, such as gold, are found in abundance.

_____ **2.** The passage establishes that gold can change its shape rather easily because it is soft.

_____ **3.** The passage establishes that heat and electricity are unable to pass through gold.

_____ **4.** The passage implies that gold's color adds to its attractiveness.

_____ **5.** The passage implies that gold will probably never be used widely in industry because it is a rare substance.

When two people each have goods that the other wants, they can make a simple trade in a transaction known as **bartering**. Indeed, this is how people and even countries conducted business for many years. Because this system was not entirely satisfactory, banks and governments began to make coins which served as an exchangeable equivalent for these goods and services. The earliest coins were made of precious metals such as silver and gold. The value of these metals was fixed and agreed upon internationally. A **gold standard** was established, and most international payments were made in gold. The United States abolished the gold standard in 1934. After World War II, a new international monetary system was established.

_____ **6.** The passage establishes that the existence of gold has been known for a long time.

_____ **7.** The passage establishes that bartering is not practiced today at all.

_____ **8.** The passage implies that gold and silver are not the only metals considered to be precious.

_____ **9.** The passage implies that coins formed from gold and silver preceded coins made from other metals.

_____ **10.** The passage implies that World War II had something to do with why the gold standard was dropped.

In a South African basin called Witwatersrand or "Rand" for short, approximately two-thirds of the world's supply of gold is mined. Miners risk their lives by going 10,000 feet and more under the surface of the earth to extract gold found in layers only a few feet thick but miles long. At these depths, temperatures often exceed 120 degrees Fahrenheit, making air cooling of the shafts a necessity.

_____ **11.** The passage establishes that most of the world's gold is mined in South Africa.

_____ **12.** The passage establishes that South Africa exports gold.

_____ **13.** The passage implies that gold is commonly found near the surface of the earth.

_____ **14.** The passage implies that gold is not equally distributed in the world.

_____ **15.** The passage implies that gold mining is a dangerous endeavor.

Between 1848 and 1852, the population of the area known today as California grew from 15,000 to 250,000, an astonishing rate of increase in those days. What drew people to this region was "gold fever." Most gold was found in streams and rivers in small solid pieces called "nuggets." Nuggets were often separated from sand and gravel through a process known as "panning." In this process, a pan was filled with material found in the river beds or dug out of the ground. Water was added, and the pan was shaken. When the water was poured out, the lighter sand and gravel went with it. The heavier gold nuggets, if there were any, stayed behind in the bottom of the pan.

People who pulled up their roots in hopes of finding their fortunes were called "49ers," because 1849 was the year of the greatest migration. Many 49ers came by ship, but most traveled by covered wagon across the Oregon Trail or the California Trail. Existing settlements were inadequate for the great influx, so new towns sprang up almost overnight. By 1850, California had enough people to qualify for statehood.

_____ **16.** The passage establishes that in California gold was located on the surface of the earth.

_____ **17.** The passage establishes that panning was not an effective means of discovering gold.

_____ **18.** The passage establishes that if gold is found on the surface, it will also be found deep in the earth.

_____ **19.** The passage implies that at least some 49ers became rich.

_____ **20.** The passage implies that California has an active gold-mining industry today.

Exercise B Using what you have learned from the information presented in the preceding exercise, answer the following questions.

1. What are two methods of extracting gold from the earth? What are the advantages and disadvantages of each.

2. Which of gold's properties make it an attractive metal for coins? Which make it unattractive?

3. The price of gold has fluctuated greatly in recent times. In the late 1970s, one ounce cost as much as $800, yet five years later the same amount was selling for $250. What factors might account for this?

4. At one time, international payments were made in gold. What properties of gold make this an inefficient way of paying bills?

5. "Rand" has several meanings. From one of the preceding passages you learned that this word is a shortened form of "Witwatersrand." "Rand" is also the name of the money used in South Africa. Speculate as to why the same word refers both to a geographical location and to the South African currency.

Exercise C The following passages come from physics, physiology, psychology, and comparative sociology. In them, you will study various aspects on the topic of "color." After each passage are comprehension questions that require an answer of <u>true</u> or <u>false</u>.

Colors and Wavelengths

Whether from the sun or an electric lamp, light makes it possible for us to see colors. Light is composed of various types of rays of energy called **waves**, each of which is a different length. The longest wavelength of light visible to the human eye is seen as red, followed by orange, yellow, green, blue, and violet respectively. Combinations of these wavelengths produce variations of these basic colors.

The list of colors produced by differing wavelengths excludes black and white. This is because these two cases are special. When equal amounts of all colors are combined, they are seen as white. Conversely, when no colors are present, we see black. White, then, is a mixture of all colors while black is the absence of them.

_____ **1.** The passage identifies two sources of light.

_____ **2.** The passage establishes that without light, we would be unable to see.

_____ **3.** What distinguishes one wavelength from another is how long it is.

_____ **4.** The passage implies that there are wavelengths we cannot see.

_____ **5.** Green wavelengths are shorter than orange ones.

_____ **6.** Six basic colors are identified in the passage.

_____ **7.** The passage establishes how many combinations of wavelengths are possible.

_____ **8.** The number of combinations of wavelengths is probably quite large.

_____ **9.** The passage establishes that black is the opposite of white.

_____**10.** The passage implies that in a technical sense black is not a color.

Selective Reflection

We can see an object only when a light shines on it. The surface of a particular object will absorb some of this light's wavelengths and reflect others. This process is known as **selective reflection**. The color we see is the color that is reflected. To illustrate this, let us consider the colors of a tree. The leaves appear green because all other wavelengths of the light hitting them are absorbed. The trunk of a tree appears brown because brown is the only wavelength which is reflected.

The only two colors we see that are not the product of selective reflection are black and white. When a surface absorbs all the wavelengths of a light source, that surface appears black. When it absorbs none, it appears white.

_____ **11.** The passage defines wavelengths.

_____ **12.** The passage explains why some surfaces absorb certain wavelengths and reflect others.

_____ **13.** The word "selective" implies that only some wavelengths are reflected.

_____ **14.** Leaves look green to us because this color is absorbed while all others are reflected.

_____ **15.** The trunk of a tree appears brown because this color is reflected.

_____ **16.** White does not reflect light selectively; it reflects all lightwaves.

_____ **17.** An object will appear black because no wavelengths are reflected.

_____ **18.** An object will appear white when all the colors from a light source are reflected from that object's surface.

_____ **19.** The six basic colors identified in the preceding passage are probably all subject to the selective reflection process.

_____ **20.** The page of this book reflects all the light that is shining on it, but the words on the page absorb all the light.

Color Blindness

Approximately 8% of all males and 0.5% of all females do not have full ability to see the normal range of colors. This condition, which nearly always manifests itself from birth, is known as **achromatopsia** or more commonly as color blindness.

Located in the inner eye is the retina which contains **cones** and **rods**. The former help us see various colors while the latter enable us to see in dim light, but only blacks, grays, and whites. The eyes of certain animals contain only rods, indicating that these animals are color blind. The eyes of most animals that are active during the day, however, contain both cones and rods. These animals are said to have color vision.

In rare cases, people can be totally color blind. This happens when the cones are non-functioning. Most common is red-green blindness, which makes it impossible to distinguish between red and green.

_____ **21.** Nearly one out of every ten people are affected by achromotopsia.

_____ **22.** The passage explains why more men than women are affected by achromotopsia.

_____ **23.** Achromotopsia is synonymous with color blindness.

_____ **24.** Color blindness can develop later in life.

_____ **25.** The retina is made up of at least two parts.

_____ **26.** Cones register colors and rods register blacks, whites and grays.

_____ **27.** The passage implies that animals which are active at night generally have rods only.

_____ **28.** Cats are active during the day and therefore probably have both cones and rods.

_____ **29.** There are people who can only see various shades of black, gray, and white.

_____ **30.** People who are color blind are able to see one color only.

Colors and Culture

In almost every culture, particular colors symbolize particular emotions. The emotions they stand for, however, vary from culture to culture. In China, for example, happiness and joy are associated with the color red. In Egypt, these feelings are tied to yellow. Green communicates power to Egyptians, but to the Japanese it is associated with youth. To English-speaking North Americans, green brings to mind jealousy or inexperience, red connotes anger, yellow may mean caution or cowardice, and blue can summon up feelings of sadness.

The standardization of traffic lights throughout the world is probably affecting the traditional views of red, yellow, and green in cultures where they might have other meanings. Red, of course, is a signal to stop, yellow indicates caution, and green means to proceed freely.

_____ **31.** The passage establishes that all colors evoke certain emotions within a culture.

_____ **32.** The words "emotions" and "feelings" are used interchangeably in the passage.

_____ **33.** The passage establishes that people from all cultures are able to distinguish the six basic colors.

_____ **34.** In both Japan and Egypt, green is associated with feelings that are probably positive. In North America, however, green is associated with feelings that are probably negative.

_____ **35.** It is possible that even within a culture, one color can have several associations.

_____ **36.** The passage suggests that there are rational reasons why cultures associate certain emotions with certain colors.

_____ **37.** The passage suggests that the retina's cones and rods might vary from culture to culture.

_____ **38.** The passage establishes the usefulness of a universally-observed system of traffic lights.

_____ **39.** The passage implies that red, yellow, and green might not be the natural choice of traffic light signals in all cultures.

_____ **40.** It is possible that in some cultures, green is associated with danger.

Colors and Emotions

Studies have revealed that people react in different ways to different colors. For example, humans tend to become more excited when exposed to red light and more passive with blue light. Interestingly, pink, which is closer to red than to blue, seems to be the most soothing color of all. This finding has implications for interior decorators, particularly those charged with deciding which colors to paint the walls of hospitals and prisons.

_____ **41.** The passage establishes a connection between exposure to certain colors and physical responses.

_____ **42.** The passage establishes that pink is more relaxing than blue, and that blue is more soothing than red.

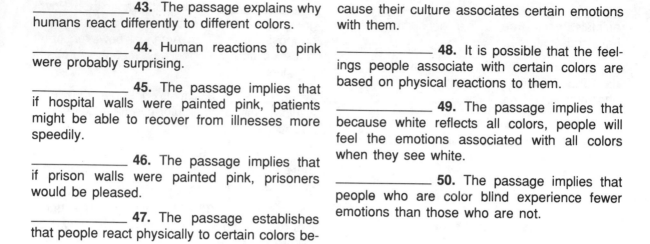

_____ **43.** The passage explains why humans react differently to different colors.

_____ **44.** Human reactions to pink were probably surprising.

_____ **45.** The passage implies that if hospital walls were painted pink, patients might be able to recover from illnesses more speedily.

_____ **46.** The passage implies that if prison walls were painted pink, prisoners would be pleased.

_____ **47.** The passage establishes that people react physically to certain colors be-cause their culture associates certain emotions with them.

_____ **48.** It is possible that the feelings people associate with certain colors are based on physical reactions to them.

_____ **49.** The passage implies that because white reflects all colors, people will feel the emotions associated with all colors when they see white.

_____ **50.** The passage implies that people who are color blind experience fewer emotions than those who are not.

Exercise D Using what you have learned from the information presented in the preceding exercise, answer the following questions.

1. Make a list of colors and the associations they have in your culture. Examine the lists of classmates from cultures other than your own and make a table showing your findings.

2. Write a paragraph explaining some of the difficulties an individual affected by color blindness might have. How might this person adjust to the problem?

3. One passage suggested that colors can affect how we react to our environment. Aside from hospitals and prisons, where else might we wish to apply the findings of this study?

4. Explain why animals that are active during the day are more likely to have color vision than animals active during the night.

5. In addition to the colors of traffic lights, what other internationally-recognized colors are there?

Exercise E The following passages are taken from archaeology, astronomy, biology, chemistry, earth science, and meteorology. By integrating information from them, you will be able to piece together two competing theories about how dinosaurs disappeared from the earth.

According to one theory, a shower of objects from space hit the earth, setting in action a causal chain. The second theory holds that volcanoes were ultimately responsible for the dinosaurs' extinction.

Try to think of yourself as a detective solving a mystery as you select and integrate information from these passages. Your assignment is to find evidence to support these two theories. Each passage is followed by a set of comprehension questions which require an answer of <u>true</u> or <u>false</u>.

Dinosaurs

Until 65 million years ago, a family of animals known as **dinosaurs** roamed the earth. Dinosaurs were for the most part terrestrial reptiles, meaning they lived on land, and had skins covered with scales. Some dinosaurs were carnivorous (meat-eating) while others were herbivorous (plant-eating). Dinosaurs disappeared at about the same time as did a large number of other groups of species, including the microscopic organisms that created the White Cliffs of Dover in England. Perhaps the reason the dinosaurs are remembered while these other organisms are not is their immense size. For example, one type of dinosaur, the brontosaurus, weighed nearly 30 tons.

_____ **1.** Dinosaurs lived for 65 million years.

_____ **2.** Some dinosaurs may have lived in water.

_____ **3.** All dinosaurs had basically the same diet.

_____ **4.** The passage implies that the dinosaur's diet may have been responsible for its extinction.

_____ **5.** The passage establishes that dinosaurs disappeared for the same reason that other organisms living at the same time did.

_____ **6.** The White Cliffs of Dover were formed at least 65 million years ago.

_____ **7.** The passage suggests that the disappearance of the dinosaur is more important than that of other organisms.

_____ **8.** A dinosaur is a type of brontosaurus.

_____ **9.** The brontosaurus was probably the only type of dinosaur which was huge.

_____ **10.** The passage offers no explanation as to why dinosaurs and other organisms became extinct.

Volcanoes

The earth consists of a number of layers, each with its own kind of solid or liquid matter. The coolest layers are found near the surface, while the hottest are found deep within the interior. The layers of the interior contain vast amounts of energy which are trapped under the layers of the exterior. Occasionally, this energy finds a release in what we call a **volcano**. A volcano erupts when the hot liquid matter known as **magma** travels upward from within the earth through breaks or **fissures** in rocks to the surface. Magma is usually accompanied by steam and other gases such as sulfur dioxide or carbon dioxide.

Volcanoes can unleash a tremendously destructive force. In 1883, for example, the Krakatoa Volcano, located between Java and Sumatra, erupted and formed a huge tidal wave which killed 36,000 people. So much gas and fine dust were released that the skies darkened for a long period, and particles of volcanic dust remained suspended high in the atmosphere for years. This particular eruption, like many others in modern times, was of short duration. There is some evidence that the Daccan Traps, located in western India, were the site of volcanoes some 66 million years ago that were active for nearly 500,000 years.

_____**11.** The cooler layers of the earth are solid, while the hotter ones are liquid.

_____**12.** A volcano, in effect, is a type of safety valve whereby pressure can be released from the earth's interior.

_____**13.** Magma originates from breaks in rocks just below the surface of the earth.

_____**14.** A fissure is another name for a break.

_____**15.** Steam is a gas.

_____**16.** Magma is composed of hot liquid matter, steam, carbon dioxide and sulfur dioxide.

_____**17.** The passage implies that volcanoes are always destructive.

_____**18.** The passage suggests that volcanoes are probably more destructive today than they were long ago.

_____**19.** If the Krakatoa Volcano could darken the skies for a long period, the Daccan Traps Volcanoes could have for a much longer time.

_____**20.** It is possible that skies darkened by volcanic gas and dust played a part in the extinction of the dinosaur.

Asteroids

Flying through space between the orbits of Jupiter and Mars are tens of thousands of rocky objects called **asteroids**. Asteroids vary in size from a few meters to 770 km in diameter. An asteroid, then, is capable of wreaking great destruction should it pass close enough to a planet to be pulled toward it by that planet's gravitational force. There is ample evidence that asteroids or pieces of them called **meteors** have indeed collided with the earth in the past. Near Winslow, Arizona, for example, is a crater nearly a mile wide which is believed to have formed when a meteor weighing one million tons crashed approximately 50,000 years ago. A hundred similar sites have been identified around the world, and scientists believe that many more have been eroded by wind and water to the point that they are no longer recognizable. Scientists feel sure that collisions between the earth and its smaller cousins occur fairly frequently.

If one large asteroid or showers of meteors hit the earth, the collision would cause many tons of dust to be lifted into the atmosphere, with the effect that the skies would be darkened for a long time.

_____**21.** The one trait that distinguishes asteroids from planets is their size.

_____**22.** Meteors and asteroids have paths that are permanently fixed.

_____**23.** Because a meteor comes from an asteroid, it too is made of rock.

_____**24.** A crater is probably a large hole in the ground.

_____**25.** A meteor weighing one million tons can be seen near Winslow, Arizona.

_____**26.** The crater at Winslow is one of about one hundred in existence in the world today.

_____**27.** We can assume that if a collision were to occur, the dust lifted into the atmosphere would come from both the earth and the asteroid/meteor.

_____**28.** It is quite possible that meteors or asteroids fell directly on all the dinosaurs, killing them instantly.

_____**29.** It is possible that the earth was struck by many meteors, causing a blackout of the skies.

_____**30.** An extended darkening of the skies caused by multiple collisions of the earth and meteors/asteroids may be related to the extinction of the dinosaur.

The Ozone Layer

The atmosphere of the earth, consisting of various gases, extends roughly 6,000 miles (10,000 km) from the surface of our planet. In a region of the upper atmosphere can be found a layer of **ozone**, a blue gaseous substance which is composed of three atoms of oxygen. (Ordinary molecules of oxygen have two atoms.) Ozone is formed when ultraviolet rays from the sun strike oxygen in the atmosphere, and convert some of it to ozone. The ozone layer, ranging 20 to 30 miles in diameter, functions to filter most of the ultraviolet rays from the sun. Without it, the full intensity of the ultraviolet rays would kill or damage life on earth.

In recent years, various threats to the ozone layer have been identified. These include sulfur dioxide, nitrogen oxides and chlorofluorocarbons. The first gas is present in increasing quantities largely owing to the burning of coal and oil, but it is also released naturally when volcanoes erupt. Nitrogen oxides are introduced into the atmosphere mainly through the exhaust of automobiles and jet aircraft. When nuclear weapons are exploded, large amounts of these gases are also released. The last, chlorofluorocarbons, are members of a family of synthetic chemicals, some of which are found in aerosol sprays, such as deodorants, and others in coolants such as Freon, the substance used in refrigeration coils and air conditioning systems.

_____**31.** An atmosphere is an area which contains gases.

_____**32.** Ozone is a form of oxygen.

_____**33.** The primary source of ultraviolet rays is the sun.

_____**34.** The ozone layer is one of the largest of the layers composing the earth's atmosphere.

_____**35.** When ultraviolet rays enter the earth's atmosphere, only some of them reach us because they are absorbed by oxygen to form ozone.

_____**36.** The passage establishes that ultraviolet rays are harmful in every way.

_____**37.** The passage implies that one consequence of living in an industrialized society may be a weakening of the ozone layer.

_____**38.** Of the three threats to the ozone layer, the combustion of oil and coal is probably the easiest to stop.

_____**39.** Sulfur dioxide, which is released when volcanoes erupt, can damage the ozone layer.

_____**40.** It is possible that massive and extensive volcanic eruptions over 65 million years ago released so much sulfur dioxide into the air that the ozone layer was severely damaged.

Acid Rain

When fossil fuels (e.g., petroleum) are burned, sulfur dioxide gas is released. Mixed with the moisture already present in the air, it readily forms poisonous sulfuric acid. Sulfuric acid combines with rainwater to create undesirable environmental effects, including the excessive corrosion of structures, the acidification of lakes and streams, and the damaging of plant and animal life. The alarming rate at which the Acropolis in Athens, Greece, is disintegrating has been attributed to sulfur dioxide. Acid rain is responsible for a high rate of fish mortality in a number of Canadian lakes. In plants, acid rain retards growth by causing yellowing, dehydration and leaf drop.

_____**41.** Sulfur dioxide is a byproduct of the combustion of petroleum.

_____**42.** Water and sulfur dioxide form sulfuric acid.

_____**43.** Water and sulfur dioxide do not mix easily.

_____**44.** The passage establishes that sulfuric acid has no beneficial uses.

_____**45.** The passage establishes that sulfuric acid in rainwater has negative effects.

_____ **46.** The passage implies that acid rain is more prevalent in industrialized countries than in non-industrialized ones.

_____ **47.** The passage implies that a country where there are many automobiles will probably be affected by acid rain.

_____ **48.** The passage implies that acid rain will continue to be a problem until cleaner fuels are developed or until methods of neutralizing sulfur dioxide can be developed.

_____ **49.** It is possible that the dinosaur disappeared owing to the burning of petroleum.

_____ **50.** It is possible that the sulfur dioxide released through volcanic activity caused acid rain which killed the dinosaur's food supply.

Iridium

Iridium, whose chemical symbol is Ir, is a rare, whitish-yellow, very hard and heavy metallic element which is related to platinum and gold. Because it is corrosion-resistant and extremely durable, iridium is particularly useful with high-temperature materials. It is only found in great concentrations in the earth's core and in asteroids, meteors, and comets.

_____ **51.** Iridium is found in the earth in abundance.

_____ **52.** Gold is yellow, so platinum is probably white.

_____ **53.** The origin of iridium is both the earth and outer space.

_____ **54.** Because iridium is found in the earth's core, a geological analysis of magma might reveal quantities of it.

_____ **55.** Because iridium is present in asteroids and meteors, it might be found near crater sites.

Photosynthesis

Green plants use sunlight to convert carbon dioxide and water into sugar and oxygen. The complicated process through which this is accomplished is called **photosynthesis**. Light is essential to this process, and the first part of its name, "photo," means "light."

_____ **56.** Plants turn carbon dioxide into sugar.

_____ **57.** The passage implies that plants are a source of oxygen.

_____ **58.** It is possible that the carbon dioxide which accompanies volcanic eruptions could be absorbed by plants.

_____ **59.** It is possible that so much dust was lifted into the atmosphere during a meteor/asteroid shower that photosynthesis was interrupted and plant life died.

_____ **60.** It is possible that volcanic dust darkened skies for such a long time that plants died owing to a lack of sunlight.

Greenhouse Effect

A greenhouse is a structure made of glass used for growing plants that require controlled humidity and temperature. These structures are commonly found in cool climates because they are able to keep the environment inside warmer than that on the outside. The atmosphere of the earth provides a **greenhouse effect** in that a large part of the heat emitted by the earth remains trapped in the atmosphere. Certain molecules in the atmosphere function like the glass of a greenhouse, helping to retain heat. Among these molecules are water, carbon dioxide, and ozone.

Should amounts of these heat-retaining molecules increase substantially, the climate of the earth would probably change. Scientists believe that the temperature would increase, causing a melting of the polar ice caps and massive flooding throughout much of the world.

_____ 61. A greenhouse would more likely be found in a country with a cold climate than in one with a hot and wet one.

_____ 62. The earth and its atmosphere are compared to a greenhouse.

_____ 63. The glass of a greenhouse is compared to the surface of the earth.

_____ 64. The passage implies that temperatures just above the earth's atmosphere are colder than those within the atmosphere.

_____ 65. The passage establishes the source of the heat that is emitted from the earth.

_____ 66. The heat that is trapped in the earth's atmosphere probably prevents temperatures from dropping much at night.

_____ 67. The passage states that water, carbon dioxide, and ozone are the principal molecules responsible for the retention of heat in the atmosphere.

_____ 68. The passage implies that if the amount of heat-retaining molecules were to decrease, temperatures would drop.

_____ 69. Information in this passage supports the theory that asteroids or meteors can contribute to a greenhouse effect.

_____ 70. It is possible that the carbon dioxide from volcanoes caused the atmosphere to retain more heat which in turn was responsible for flooding.

Geological Layers

Archaeologists and geologists have long studied rock formations to help learn more about how the earth was formed and what happened during various periods of its history. One of the best locations for conducting these investigations is outside of Gubbio, an Italian town between Florence and Rome. The rock layers at Gubbio contain a complete geological record of the time when dinosaurs disappeared from the face of the earth.

A particular layer of rock may contain the remains of organisms that lived when the rock was laid down. These remains are called **fossils**. At Gubbio, it was noticed that a layer of limestone laid down 65 million years ago contained many fossils, but none of these fossils were found in the layer covering it. Between these two layers was a thin layer of red clay. That the covering layers held none of the fossils in the lower layer indicated that these organisms became extinct during the period between the times the layers were laid down.

When the red clay layer was analyzed, significant amounts of a rare element called iridium were found in it. Because the layer was so thin, it was thought that it somehow settled on the limestone layer, much as snow might settle on the ground. Iridium-enriched red clay was also discovered at many other sites.

_____ 71. The passage implies that by analyzing rocks, we can learn about the earth's past.

_____ 72. The passage establishes that one layer of the earth may contain different types of rocks from those in another layer.

_____ 73. The passage explains how the age of a rock can be determined.

_____ 74. Fossils can be found in layers of rock containing limestone.

_____ 75. Gubbio is the only suitable location for conducting geological examinations.

_____ 76. The passage explains why so much iridium was found in a thin layer of red clay.

_____ **77.** The dusting of the earth with iridium is compared to a snowstorm.

_____ **78.** The passage leads us to believe that iridium poisoned the dinosaur and other organisms.

_____ **79.** It is possible that a layer of iridium settled over the earth after extensive volcanic activity.

_____ **80.** It is possible that a layer of iridium settled over the earth after a shower of meteors or asteroids collided with the earth.

Exercise F Using the information you have gathered from a reading of the passages in the preceding exercise, answer the following questions.

1. Explain the relationship between iridium and meteors or asteroids. Between iridium and volcanoes.

2. Explain how sulfur dioxide from volcanoes can contribute to the formation of acid rain and to a weakening of the ozone layer.

3. Explain how the clouds of dust were created when showers of meteors or asteroids collide with the earth, or when volcanoes erupt, might affect the food chain.

4. Draw a flow chart showing how a meteor shower might ultimately cause the extinction of the dinosaurs.

5. Draw a flow chart showing how a massive volcanic eruption might set into motion a causal chain leading to the disappearance of the dinosaur.

6. Write a composition comparing the two theories. In the last paragraph, take a position as to which theory you think is stronger.

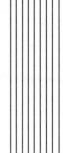

Common Abbreviations

Distance Abbreviations

in.	inch
ft.	foot
yd.	yard
m.	mile
mm.	millimeter
cm.	centimeter
m.	meter
km.	kilometer

Weight Abbreviations

oz.	ounce
lb.	pound
mg.	milligram
kg.	kilogram

Time Abbreviations

sec.	second
min.	minute
hr.	hour
wk.	week
mo.	month
yr.	year

am, a.m., AM the hours after midnight and before noon

pm, p.m., PM the hours after noon and before midnight

Quantity Abbreviations

pt.	pint
qt.	quart
gal.	gallon
ml.	milliliter
l.	liter
cc, c.c.	cubic centimeter(s)

Direction Abbreviations

N	north
S	south
E	east
W	west
NE	northeast
NW	northwest
SE	southeast
SW	southwest

Organization Abbreviations

assn.	association
co.	company
corp.	corporation
inc.	incorporated
ltd.	limited
org.	organization

Assorted Abbreviations

ac, a.c.	alternating current	**amp**	ampere
dc, d.c.	direct current	**v**	volt
AM	amplitude modulation	**w**	watt
FM	frequency modulation	**sq.**	square
C	centigrade or Celsius	**c., cu.**	cubic
F	Fahrenheit		

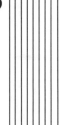

Selected Passages

The twenty passages contained in this appendix are intended to supplement activities presented in Chapters 3 through 8. Teachers may also wish to view them as core passages for further related readings from various content-area textbooks.

Passage 1, from Pathology

The first major statement on the nature of the spread of disease was written by Girolamo Fracastorio, an Italian scholar and poet. Although not trained as a doctor of medicine, he lived in a community that fell victim to an epidemic of smallpox and measles. His book, published in 1546, concluded that diseases could not spread to another person indirectly, say, through clothing. In other words, contagion was limited to person-to-person contact.

The next major advance came through the microscope. Anthony van Leeuwenhoek adapted the lens to construct a simple microscope with magnifications as great as 300 times and, more importantly, with excellent resolution which permitted observation of fine detail. This invention opened the door to a new world, especially to the world of the microbe.

Passage 2, from Meteorology

Cloud-seeding is a procedure that is thought to result in precipitation. The underlying theory is that inserting (seeding) silver iodide in a cold cloud will cause icy cloud particles to grow. Although other substances such as lead iodide and cupric sulfide have the same effect, silver iodide remains the substance most commonly used.

Although some experiments indicate that cloud-seeding does not produce rain, others suggest that under the right conditions it does indeed increase the chances of precipitation by 10 to 20 percent.

Passage 3, from Chemistry

The study of low temperatures is called **cyrogenics**. Liquid nitrogen, being easy to manufacture, is one substance used to freeze foods quickly. It has the advantage of doing this so quickly that no damage is done to the cell structure of these foods. Presumably, liquid nitrogen could be used on the human body as well. Some research is being conducted on the feasibility of freezing the bodies of people who are dying of diseases that are presently incurable and "thawing" them out at some time in the future when cures have been developed.

Passage 4, from Medical Science

Acupuncture has had medical applications for over 5,000 years. Some historians believe that acupuncture had its beginnings when during a battle in ancient China, a soldier was wounded in the hand by an arrow. Soon after, a chronic toothache ceased bothering him. This led doctors to systematically stick pins in their patients' bodies and observe the effects. More than 800 different locations were identified where the pins seemed to help the sick.

In the 1970s, contact between China and the West increased, and acupuncture was widely studied with great interest. The medical establishment in the West, though at first quite skeptical about the efficacy of this method, soon began to take acupuncture more seriously. A growing body of evidence suggests that acupuncture is an effective anesthetic or "pain killer."

Passage 5, from Human Physiology

Electrical impulses are constantly being produced throughout your nervous system. These impulses cause significant changes that are registered in the brain. The electrical activity of the brain was first observed in 1929 by a German scientist named Hans Berger, who made it possible to record brain waves without opening the skull. A record of this electrical activity is known as an **electroencephalogram** or more commonly as an **EEG**.

An EEG is administered by placing electrodes at various points on the patient's scalp. These electrodes are connected by wires to an amplifier. The output of the amplifier controls the movement of an instrument that functions like a pen writing on a moving piece of paper. This record shows different electrical patterns when the patient is excited or relaxed, drowsy or asleep. Many other physical states have also been identified.

Passage 6, from Logic

The "Law of Contradiction" is commonly attributed to Aristotle, the great Greek philosopher who lived nearly 2,500 years ago. This law is in effect a simple observation about reality. It states that a thing cannot both exist and not exist at the same time. For example, we cannot assert at the same time that Aristotle both lived and did not live. When two statements are contradictory, both cannot be true, and both cannot be false.

It is possible, of course, for two statements to be false. An example would be if we assert that all insects are harmful and that no insects are harmful. In this case, both statements cannot be true, but both can be false. Aristotle called statements such as these "contrary statements."

Furthermore, it is possible to think of statements that can both be true but that cannot both be false. Consider this pair of statements: some people are good; some people are bad. Aristotle called these types of statements "subcontrary statements."

Passage 7, from Physical Science

Nearly five hundred years ago, an English philosopher named William of Ockham formulated a rule that has found use in philosophy and science. Called **Ockham's razor**, this rule states that when there are several explanations for the same phenomenon, the simplest one is preferable.

An application of Ockham's razor can be found in the study of non-human life forms. For many years, people thought that when an animal ran away from an approaching person, it was because the animal was afraid. When a worm was put on a fishhook, people thought it felt pain. When a cat was observed feeding its young, it was thought that the cat loved its offspring. Interpretations such these are projections of human qualities onto other life forms. A simpler explanation is that the animal is responding to visual stimuli, the worm to sensory stimuli, and the cat to biological instincts. There is no proven basis for assuming that these life forms can "fear" or "feel pain" or "love."

Passage 8, from Microbiology

Everyone suffers from a cold at one time or another. Although not considered to be a serious sickness, colds do cause great discomfort. Familiar symptoms include coughing, sneezing, blocked nasal passages, and sore throat.

In the 1950's, scientists discovered that a large number of viruses were responsible for colds. At that time, it was thought that these viruses were indirectly transmitted to other people through the air, largely through coughing or sneezing. Doctors now tell us that this is not always the case. Cold viruses can indeed be passed through the air — but with difficulty. More commonly, they are passed from person to person through some sort of direct contact, for example by shaking hands.

When cold viruses (or any foreign microorganisms) enter the body, the blood manufactures a special substance called an **antibody**. Antibodies are proteins that neutralize the invaders and then remain on guard against any future attacks. If there were only one virus responsible for colds, everyone would catch a cold only one time. However, there are at least 100 different kinds of cold viruses, and this explains why people repeatedly catch colds.

Because so many virus types exist, it has been extremely difficult to develop an effective treatment for colds. If you catch a cold, doctors generally recommend that you eat healthy foods, drink plenty of liquids, and take aspirin. In addition, you can purchase products that suppress the symptoms of colds.

Passage 9, from Advertising

In 1956, a certain technique used in advertising caused quite a bit of controversy. **Subliminal advertising** made use of very short but repeated commercial messages hidden between the frames of a film. These messages were so short that few people were even consciously aware of them, yet it was claimed that they were "subliminally" communicated to the viewer.

The advertising executive responsible for the development of this technique was James Vicary, who announced at a press conference that his technique could revolutionize the advertising field. He cited an experiment he had conducted in a movie theater located in Fort Dix, New Jersey. At various points during the showing of a film, the screen flashed "Drink Coca-Cola" and "Eat popcorn." Vicary claimed that sales of both products — available in the theater lobby — increased substantially. The results of his experiment generated great interest within the advertising industry, but the public reacted quite angrily. Vicary was accused by the press and government officials of promoting "mind control."

In fact, Vicary's technique was neither new nor particularly effective. Subsequent studies with better controls in place showed that subliminal suggestions are effective only (1) when information on the conscious level is insufficient to help us make a decision, and (2) when we are highly motivated to follow a "hunch."

Passage 10, from Mathematics

Nearly all countries in the world today, including the United States, officially use the metric system of measurement. In the United states, however, another system is also used officially. This is the English or customary system.

The metric system, invented in France about 200 years ago, is largely a decimal system, with units related to each other in multiples of ten. (An exception to this is the measurement of time, in which 60 seconds equal one minute, 60 minutes equal one hour, and 24 hours equal one day.)

The English or customary system is based on arbitrary measurements established many centuries ago in England. For example, the foot was originally the average length of an adult human foot. In the 17th century it was standardized as the length of the foot of King James I. The inch was one twelfth of the foot; the yard was three feet; the rod was $16\frac{1}{2}$ feet; the mile was 320 rods — or 1760 yards or 5280 feet! In contrast, the metric system was based on a known distance on the surface of the earth, and all other measurements were related to it in multiples of ten.

In the United States, the metric system is used almost exclusively in science. It is also used widely in many industries, including automobile manufacturing. Packaged foods and some beverages are usually labeled with both English and metric weights or capacities. Most Americans, however, continue to measure distances in inches, feet, yards, and miles rather than in millimeters, centimeters, meters, and kilometers, and to pump their motor fuel in gallons rather than in liters.

Many persons feel that the use of the metric and English systems side by side produces unnecessary confusion. They believe that because the metric system is already used by a majority of the world's population and because the English system is so troublesome mathematically, the latter should be completely discarded in favor of the former.

Passage 11, from Statistics

The United Nations designated June 10, 1987 as the day when the world population reached the five billion mark. More than five billion people now live on this planet.

Nearly two thousand years ago, the population of the earth was probably somewhere around 250 million people. By 1975, the four billion mark was reached. The growth from so few to so many did not happen gradually. In fact, in 1820, estimates placed the number of the earth's inhabitants at only one billion. One hundred years later, the number doubled to two billion. At present rates of growth, projections of a world population of six billion by the turn of this century have been made (U.S. Department of Commerce 1979). In order to understand how populations grow, the concept of **doubling time** must be understood.

For the population to grow from 250 million to 500 million, almost 1,700 years were required. From one to two billion took 110 years. Two became four billion in only 45 years. At the present growth rate of 1.8 percent per year, the doubling time is a mere 35 years.

Passage 12, from Business

The Great Depression took place in the 1930s in the United States. At that time, a man in Jamaica, New York, named Michael Kullen opened a grocery store which was nearly seven times larger than the typical grocery store. This store had the added novelty of allowing customers to serve themselves and pay a cashier. The high sales volume that the size of his store permitted as well as Kullen's self-service system enabled him to undercut the prices of his competitors. Thus, the first "supermarket" was born. The idea quickly spread, and within ten years nearly 5,000 such supermarkets sprang up across the United States.

The success of these enterprises had a considerable impact on the way retailers do business. The cornerstone of the approach, self-service, was widely adapted to other stores selling such items as hardware, clothing, and general merchandise. The other important feature—that of large scale—was also imitated. The result was that customers could be offered wider choices of products at lower prices.

Passage 13, from Chemistry

The term "organic" is quite loosely associated today with anything that is "natural." In chemistry, organic substances are defined as those which are made from carbon compounds.

Organic food is grown on organic farms, meaning that no synthetic substances are used. Common organic substances include certain fertilizers such as manure (of animal origin), compost (of plant origin) and pulverized rocks rich in various elements that provide nutrients for plants. Organic farmers avoid using artificially produced fertilizers.

From a purely chemical point of view, there is no difference between compounds that are mined directly from the earth and those that are synthetically manufactured in plants. To label the latter substances as "unnatural" is to admit ignorance of basic chemistry.

Two problems do surface, however, with non-organic farming. The first is that too much fertilizer is sometimes used. When this happens, the fertilizer eventually reaches the water supply causing an upset in the ecological balance. The second problem arises when chemical pesticides are used extensively. These poisons also eventually contaminate the water supply. They also may remain on the plants that are sprayed and may poison persons and animals that eat these plants.

Passage 14, from Astronomy

If life has come about on this planet, is it possible that it can be found elsewhere in the universe? Many scientists can find no reason to answer "no" to this question. In fact, the sheer immensity of the universe suggests that it would be unreasonable to think that life is limited to one planet in one minor solar system.

The universe contains trillions of stars. A great number of these stars have planetary systems. It is on these planets that any life would be found. If we assume that life elsewhere is similar to life here on earth, then we could expect to find it only on planets with moderate temperatures. Those planets must also be a certain size in order to have a suitable atmosphere to support life. For any number of other reasons, the vast majority of planets in the universe cannot be expected to have life forms. Despite all these considerations, however, it is estimated that there are at least one hundred million planets that might support life.

This number suggests the statistical probability of life on other planets. The question of how advanced those life forms are is something altogether different, and few scientists are willing to make any guesses. Nonetheless, a growing number of scientists supports the idea of building radio receivers to pick up any signals from outer space.

Passage 15, from Oceanography

Marine pollution is commonly associated with oil spills, sewage disposal, and industrial waste products. In short, we tend to view pollution as a condition brought about by human activity of one sort or another. To a marine biologist, however, marine pollution also brings to mind volcanic eruptions, earthquakes, and the like.

In order to combat marine pollution, biologists first need to agree on whether or not a certain substance is always to be thought of as a pollutant. Consider the example of phosphorus, which is present in industrial and human wastes.

When this chemical enters our water supplies, it is consumed by algae and plankton. These organisms, in turn, are eaten by fish and other marine life. Phosphorus, then, is not a pollutant because it plays a vital and beneficial role in the food chain.

However, as levels of phosphorus in water supplies increase, so does the number of algae and plankton. These organisms take oxygen from the water, and without oxygen most marine life will die. Phosphorus, then, is most definitely a pollutant because its effects are harmful.

Or is it? As we have seen, phosphorus is beneficial in small quantities because it increases the food supply for certain types of marine life. In large quantities, however, it indirectly kills other forms of marine life. This example should make it clear that certain substances are not fundamentally pollutants.

Passage 16, from Architecture

No building has ever been erected that is entirely earthquake-proof. The costs of doing so would be prohibitively great. The practical goal of architects is to design buildings that are earthquake-resistant. In other words, architects design structures which at best will withstand severe earthquakes and which at the very least will permit any occupants sufficient time to exit before these buildings collapse.

When building in an earthquake zone, architects and structural engineers exercise great care in the selection of the site, the materials to be used, and the design of the building itself. Factors to be considered in the location of the building include the properties of the soil and the proximity of the building to other buildings.

In general, a solid rock foundation is preferred to soft ground because seismic waves pass through the former in short jolts and through the latter in long, rocking waves. The potential for damage is greater when the ground is soft, as in Mexico City which rests on a clay bed.

Tall buildings should not be located close to each other. During an earthquake, skyscrapers will sway. Should one brush against another even slightly, the result would be disastrous for both.

The choice of materials depends on the type of building. Steel is the material of first choice for high- and medium-rise buildings, but concrete reinforced with steel runs a close second. The most suitable material for low-rise buildings is wood. Brick and stone should be avoided with all three types of buildings. This is because masonry consists of many small pieces which tend to fall apart and crumble during an earthquake.

The design of an earthquake-resistant building is of paramount importance. The best shapes are those that are simple and symmetrical, such as a square. The worst shapes are those that are tall or long. Buildings with connecting wings are also to be avoided, in particular those shaped like a "T" or an "L."

Passage 17, from Archaeology

Archaeologists are able to determine the age of certain objects through application of a technique known as **radiocarbon dating**. To understand this process, we need first to understand the role carbon plays.

In the upper atmosphere, nitrogen-14 atoms are constantly bombarded by cosmic rays. The product, carbon-14, then mixes with oxygen to form carbon dioxide. Because carbon dioxide enters and leaves all living things at the same rate, archaeologists know how much carbon-14 is present in objects when they are living.

When an object dies, no more carbon dioxide enters it. However, carbon-14 continues to decay into nitrogen at predictable rates. By measuring the amount of carbon-14 present in a dead object and comparing this amount to the amount found in a similar living object, scientists can estimate the dead object's age.

A problem with this dating technique is that a large sample of an object is required in order to administer the test. This sample is destroyed by the test procedure. Archaeologists, in short, must choose between having the object or having a date for it. One way of solving this difficulty is by dating a valueless object found near a valuable one (e.g., a piece of charcoal found where a tool made from animal bone was found). Although this solution is not always without error, it has been found to be satisfactory in most cases.

Passage 18, from Immunology

The war against illness has seen countless battles. Historically, the weapons used have been specifically designed to counter particular diseases. For example, one weapon developed to defeat certain types of bacterial infections is penicillin. Hundreds of other drugs for hundreds of other diseases fill the shelves of pharmacies, waiting to be called into battle. Though most are effective weapons, many have side effects. Penicillin, for example, produces allergic reactions in some patients.

This approach to waging war depends upon a strategy of counterattack. That is to say, only after an individual becomes sick is an offensive mounted. Advances in the branch of medicine called immunology may change the nature of this war.

Immunology — the study of how the body protects itself — is a relatively new field. Knowledge of how the immmune system works has come largely through the development of powerful microscopes and improved laboratory techniques. Immunologists hope that through their efforts we may someday be able to boost the body's immune system to a point where people simply will never become sick. If this happens, defense will make counterattack unnecessary.

The first task of the immunologists was to study how the body naturally defends itself against attack. This process is now fairly well known.

The blood of a healthy human contains both white and red cells. The former number approximately one trillion and constitute the army which protects us when foreign particles invade the body. The body constantly manufactures white blood cells in bone marrow.

Examination of these white blood cells has revealed that they fall into two basic groups: phagocytes and lymphocytes. Each type can be further divided (see Figure 18.1), and each type performs different functions.

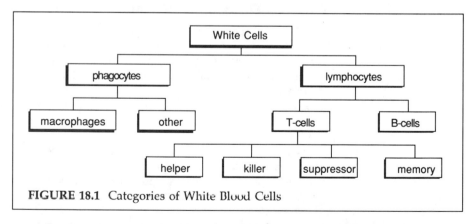

FIGURE 18.1 Categories of White Blood Cells

One type of phagocyte, the macrophage, functions like radar. Macrophages circulate around the bloodstream. After locating an enemy, these cells send out a signal to one type of lymphocyte called the T-helper cell. The T-helper cells sound the general alarm. This alarm mobilizes T-killer cells and B-cells which attack the enemy. Powerful chemicals called antibodies are used in this attack. When the battle has been won, T-suppressor cells stop the fighting. T-memory cells, manufactured specifically to fight a similar type of attack, will circulate in the bloodstream for years thereafter. Figure 18.2 condenses the entire battle plan.

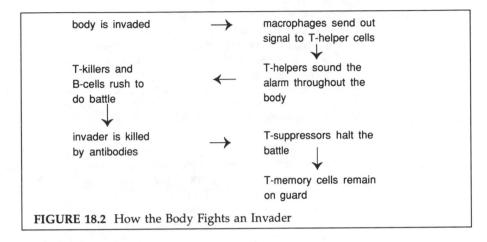

FIGURE 18.2 How the Body Fights an Invader

Passage 19, from Marketing

The purpose of a trademark is to protect both the owner and the public from deception. Neither wants products on the market that claim to be something they are not. Thus, if a customer specifies a **Walkman**, the order had better be placed with Sony. If **Jacuzzi** is named, it had better be the real thing and not just any brand of whirlpool bath.

The legal protection extended to trademarks varies from country to country. In the United States alone, nearly a half-million trademarks are registered with the Patent Office under guidelines established by the Lantham Act of 1946. By filing a trademark, manufacturers are afforded certain advantages, paramount of which is protection from infringement by other parties for as long as the mark is used. However, when a trademark falls under generic siege, that is, when it begins to be used to name a kind of product or process rather than a specific one, then the responsibility falls squarely upon the owner to do battle to protect rights to the name. This can be both costly and at times futile. The manufacturers of **Coke**, **Kleenex**, **Xerox**, **Jell-O**, **Jeep**, and **Scotch Tape** have all gone to court at one time or another to defend their brand names from going generic. They have to date been successful. Other companies have fared worse. King-Sealy, for instance, lost its exclusive right to use the word **Thermos** when surveys showed that most of the public thought this product meant any vacuum sealed bottle. The du Pont Company lost its exclusive right to the name **Cellophane** because this was the only name by which this product could be identified by the public. Other losers include aspirin, kerosene, celluloid, nylon, and lanolin. Unresolved are court cases involving Cyanamid Corporation's **Formica** and Borden's **ReaLemon**.

Is a trademark owner wholly defenseless against a public all too ready to absorb these words into common usage? Not entirely. One strategy widely employed is for manufacturers to use their trademark as a proper adjective. Thus, **Jell-O** is promoted as **Jell-O** gelatin, and **Band-Aid** as **Band-Aid** bandages. Another strategy is to make trademarks distinguishable from common nouns by encasing them in quotations or by printing them in boldface or italics. Most common is to capitalize the first letter. Certain brands have added protection by altering normal spellings and using capital letters in unlikely places, as in **Re-aLemon** and **TelePrompTer**.

One reason certain manufacturers have lost battles with the public is because the brand name itself may be especially prone to the generic process. Names that are highly descriptive of the product, for example, are particularly difficult to protect legally, and the following erstwhile trademarks have all long since gone generic: shredded wheat, dry ice, milk of magnesia, mineral oil, launderette, corn flakes, mimeograph, and phonograph. Another vulnerable group consists of semi-descriptive or suggestive names. These include cellophane, escalator, granola, and zipper.

Another reason for the popularity of a particular name is suggested by the observation that we generally prefer to use a simpler expression rather than a longer, more complex one. This 'Principle of Least Effort' may well explain why many of us will say **Band-Aid** and not "adhesive bandage," **Vaseline** and not "petroleum jelly," **Q-Tip** and not "cotton swab," **Kleenex** and not "facial tissue," **Scotch** and not "cellophane tape," **Sanka** and not "decaffeinated coffee," and **Teflon** and not tongue-twisting "polytetrafluoroethylene coating." It simply is easier to use the brand name.

One curious aspect of the generic phenomenon is an occasional grammatical shift in usage. Verb forms are not uncommon: to **Xerox** something, to **Hoover** a floor, to **White Out** a mistake, to **Wang** a document, to **Thermofax**, **Rapifax**, or **Omnifax** something, and to **Mace** someone.

The number of trademarks currently under grievous assault is difficult to ascertain. The following words comprise only a partial listing: **Ace Bandage**, **Astroturf**, **Baggie**, **Band-Aid**, **Betamax**, **Chapstick**, **Chiclets**, **Clorox**, **Coca-Cola**, **Crockpot**, **Dacron**, **Dictaphone**, **Dixie Cup**, **Formica**, **Freon**, **Frisbee**, **Frogurt**, **Hovercraft**, **Hoverpad**, **Hovertrain**, **Jacuzzi**, **Jeep**, **Jell-O**, **Kleenex**, **Laundromat**, **Mace**, **Magic Marker**, **Muzak**, **Pampers**, **Parcheesi**, **Ping-Pong**, **Plexiglas**, **Popsicle**, **Q-Tips**, **Realtor**, **Scotch Tape**, **Sheetrock**, **Styrofoam**, **Tabasco Sauce**, **T.V. Dinner**, **Technicolor**, **Teflon**, **Teletype**, **Vaseline**, **Visine**, **Walkman**, **WATS Line**, **Windbreaker**, **Windex**, **Winnebago**, and **Xerox**.

A good number from the above list have already found homes in dictionaries, where they are indeed identified as trademarks. Their inclusion, however, serves notice that many of them are probably already considered as candidates for generic use by the public if not by the lexicographer.

Passage 20, from Criminology

In the early part of the twentieth century, a Frenchman named Edmond Locard observed that criminals will always leave a trace of their presence at the scene of the crime, and that they will also always take with them some evidence that they had been at the scene of the crime. The task of people involved in law enforcement is to find that evidence. Until recently, police have had to rely on a limited number of tools to do this.

In recent times, however, discoveries in chemistry, biology, physics, and other fields have been applied to criminology, making the task of law enforcement officers a bit easier. A number of these discoveries will be discussed briefly here.

When arson, the deliberate destruction of property by fire, was suspected, police traditionally had to locate from the remains traces of the fuel used to start the fire. This sample was boiled in water and the steam collected. The fumes were then analyzed. The whole process was largely inefficient, not only because it was time-consuming but because the sample was also destroyed. Now, a substance called **Tenax**, developed at NASA for use in spacecraft, can be utilized.

Tenax can detect the presence of extremely small amounts of chemicals. An additional advantage is that the sample need not be heated (and consequently destroyed) when it undergoes analysis. The process is outlined as follows:

1. Chemical sample vaporizes naturally.
2. Vapors are absorbed by Tenax.
3. Tenax is heated.
4. Vapors are released and captured.
5. Gases are passed through a column containing various substances that absorb certain gases.
6. Gases are separated and identified.

In the case of murder by gun, police have had to compare the markings of a bullet with those in the barrel of a gun. Because the interiors of guns are now especially smooth, any matching has become exceedingly difficult. Help has come in the form of the **electron microscope**. These powerful instruments are able to detect even the smallest of imperfections of a gun's interior. The electron microscope can also be used to analyze the chemical composition of gunpowder, which will vary significantly. By examining gunpowder deposits on a suspect's clothing, police have been able to match murderers to their guns.

Another traditional method of matching criminals to their crimes has been through the use of fingerprinting. The scene of the crime is dusted. The fingerprints of suspects are then taken to determine whether or not they were present at the scene of the crime. Nowadays, the laser can be used to read fingerprints. Even if a criminal uses gloves when committing a crime or if the surface to be read is wet, lasers can help.

Even more exciting is a process called **genetic fingerprinting**, which makes use of DNA (deoxyribonucleic acid), the molecules controlling heredity. Because every cell in an individual contains the same genetic code, police can determine whether or not a suspect was present at the scene of a crime by analyzing samples of human fluids and tissues found at the scene of the crime and those of a suspect.

A technique known as **neutron-activation analysis** can help in cases concerning death under suspicious circumstances. By examining one strand of hair, police can determine which chemicals have been introduced into the body. They can also even arrive at a good guess as to when these chemicals were introduced. Suppose that Mr. X has decided to use arsenic to poison Mr. Y. Over several weeks, the murderer gives his victim small doses of arsenic placed in coffee. The hair will absorb and permanently retain traces of the poison. Mr. Y's hair provides a chemical history of his own diet — a record police can use in their investigations.

Perhaps the most useful aid in law enforcement has come from computers because they are able to scan vast amounts of information at astonishing rates.

Certain criminals have a particular signature, meaning that they commit the same crime in the same way again and again. Computers can easily compile a list of suspects by searching through memory banks for these patterns.

Computers can also render helpful information in matching substances with their manufacturers. Suppose, for instance, that a piece of glass from a headlight and some paint from a car have been found at the scene of an automobile accident. The car is nowhere to be found. After analyzing both and running this information through a computer, police can generate a short list of cars fitting this description as well as their owners. Computer programs can even be used in voice recognition and handwriting analysis.

Locard's principle still applies to criminals. Only the methods used in gathering evidence against them has changed greatly.

Glossary

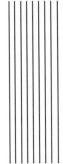

This glossary gives the meanings of words as they are used in this book. Some of the words also have other meanings.

abbreviation Shortened form of a word which is used in place of the whole. See **acronym**.

acknowledgments Section at the beginning of books in which the author expresses gratitude to those who helped in the writing of the book.

acronym A pronounceable word formed from the first (or first few) letters of major words in a term or expression; used as an abbreviation.

analogy Correspondence between two things which otherwise are different.

antonym Word that has the opposite meaning of another word. See **synonym**.

appendix Supplementary section at the end of a book containing detailed information that the author does not choose to include in the body of the book.

assumption Unsaid statement accepted without proof.

asterisk Star-shaped symbol that refers reader to page bottom for additional information.

author Person who writes a book.

bar graph Type of illustration which compares quantities through the use of rectangles of various lengths.

boldface Dark print used in reading passages to highlight important information.

boxed-in readings Short readings that are related but not essential to information in the body of the text. These readings are enclosed in a "box."

capitalizing Writing a word in capital letters; sometimes used to introduce important information.

causal chain A series of connected events, each action occurring because of the action immediately preceding it.

chapter Basic unit of a book. Each chapter covers a different area of the subject.

chart General type of illustration which gives information in rows and columns of print.

chronological order Order in which a series of events occurred.

contents. See **table of contents**.

cross-reference Instruction in one place in a reading for the reader to go to another place for relevant information.

ellipsis Omission of words that are unnecessary for an understanding of a sentence.

endnotes Explanatory or other supplementary identifying material found at the end of a chapter or book.

entry Word or term that is defined in a dictionary or glossary or that is listed in an index.

fact Statement that is widely accepted and for which proof exists.

field label A label in front of a dictionary definition which identifies the area of study that the definition applies to.

flow chart Illustration that shows the sequence of steps in a process.

footnotes Explanatory information found at the bottom of a page.

foreword See **introduction**.

generalization Statement about a class of things, based on observation of many individual members of the class or occurrences.

glossary Section that defines key words used in a text.

graph Type of illustration showing numerical relationships or data.

illustration Picture or diagram that explains or clarifies something.

implication Something suggested or indirectly expressed.

index Alphabetical listing of subjects, topics or people and the pages in the book where they are discussed; found at back of book.

integration Combining or organizing of information to form a whole from many parts.

introduction First section of a book which contains information about the purpose, background, value and/or use of that book. Sometimes called foreword or preface.

italics Slanted print sometimes used to introduce important words or terms. See also **boldface**, **capitalizing**.

lesson See **chapter**.

line graph Illustration in which a line that connects a series of dots is used to show the direction and movement of something over a period of time.

list A series of words or other items, usually having a common characteristic and presented in order.

margin Empty space between the writing on a page and the edge of the page.

metaphoric language Language implying a comparison in which a word or phrase normally found in one context (usually a familiar one) is used in another (usually an unfamiliar one).

notes in margin Brief comments or explanations found beside the reading in some textbooks.

opinion Statement of personal belief for which no or little proof exists.

organization chart Illustration in which the structure of an organization is shown.

organization marker Word(s) that signal to readers the structure of a reading.

overview See **summary**.

paragraph Subdivision of a writing which consists of one or more sentences and begins on a new (and usually indented) line.

pie chart Illustration in which a whole circle is divided into slices or parts to show the relative sizes or magnitudes of the several parts of the whole.

preface See **introduction**.

process Series of actions leading to a particular end or product.

references Alphabetized list of publications found at end of each chapter or at end of book. These publications are the source of information that is referred to in the book.

review questions Set of problems or questions found at the end of a chapter which are designed to test understanding and provide practice of the points discussed in that chapter.

section Basic subdivision of a chapter, often titled and numbered.

study objectives Set of statements found at the beginning of chapters which indicate what students should be able to do upon finishing that chapter.

subsection Basic subdivison of a section. Subsections usually have titles and sometimes are numbered as well.

substitution Replacing of one word with another, especially pronouns for nouns.

summary Outline of the major points presented or taught in a chapter.

superordinate Word representing a general class of words.

superscript Raised number or symbol found at the end of a sentence which refers the reader either to the bottom of the page or to the end of the chapter or book for an identification or clarification of information presented in the sentence.

symbol A sign that represents something.

synonym One word with approximately the same meaning as another.

table Type of illustration in which information is arranged in rows and columns usually in a rectangular shape.

table of contents List of chapters (and sometimes their subsections) together with the number of the first page of each chapter/section; it is found at the beginning of a book.

timeline Type of illustration listing a series of events in chronological order.

title Identifying name given to a book or a chapter.

title page Page at the beginning of a book on which the title of the book, the author's name, the name of the publisher, and the place of publication can be found.

underlining The use of a line under certain words to emphasize important information.

unit See **chapter**.

vocabulary list Set of the key words which were introduced in a chapter. Vocabulary lists are located at the end of a chapter.

References

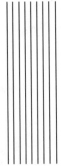

Carrell, Patricia. 1985. Facilitating ESL reading by teaching text structure. *TESOL Quarterly* 19(4):727-752.

Elson, Nicholas. 1984. Reading and meaning for university level ESL students. *TESL Talk* 15(3):26-34.

Nuttall, Christine. 1982. *Teaching Reading Skills in a Foreign Language*. London: Heinnemann Educational Books.

U.S. Department of Commerce. Bureau of the Census. 1979. New census bureau projections show world population could exceed 6 billion by the year 2000. *Commerce News* 79(38):1-2.

Answer Key

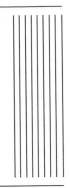

The following are answers to the odd-numbered questions of the exercises found at the end of each chapter.

Chapter 1

A.
1. level
3. level
5. 0
7. level
9. 0

B.
1. conceptually
3. conceptually
5. chronologically
7. chronologically
9. conceptually

C.
1. 78-79
3. Food Chains
5. 487

D. Answers will vary depending on text chosen.

Chapter 2

A.
1. arbitrage
3. acculturation
5. empirical formula
7. community
9. deduction, syllogism, syllogistic reasoning
major premise, minor premise, conclusion

B. Answers will vary depending on text chosen.

Chapter 3

A.
1a. camera
b. lenses
c. rays of light
3a. wheel
b. hub
c. spoke
5a. chemical symbols = letters of alphabet
b. formulas = words

7a. earth = orange
 b. lithosphere = orange peel
9a. battery = living organism
 b. voltage regulator = enzyme
B. 1. j
 3. h
 5. c
 7. a
 9. e
C. 1.

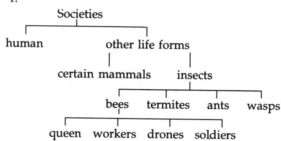

3. Answers will vary depending on your own society.
5. Answers will vary. The schistosome life cycle might be broken by avoiding disposing of human wastes in water used for other purposes.
7. Answers will vary. Rural areas are less likely to have sewage treatment plants which separate water containing human wastes from water used for other purposes.

Chapter 4

A. 1. <u>then</u>, restatement
 3. <u>in short</u>, restatement
 5. <u>conclusion</u>, determination
B. 1. [What is important for us to see here] <u>is</u> that it is sometimes difficult to find the subject and verb of a sentence.
 3. [That large bubbles formed within the liquid and rose to the surface] <u>indicates</u> that the liquid was boiling.
 5. [That all systems operate according to general principles, such as feedback,] <u>is</u> certain.
 7. [Where the implications of the study may lead] <u>is</u> seen as the most exciting phase of the projects.
 9. [For gold to have been the international monetary standard for as long as it was] <u>attests</u> to the value people universally assign it.
C. 1. noun   7. noun   13. noun
 3. adjective   9. verb   15. adjective
 5. verb   11. verb
D. 1. The waves pound on the shore endlessly and ruthlessly, continuously reshaping the coastline.

3. A company can lose millions of investment dollars if it happens that a product fails to sell.
5. One of the most important archaeological finds of the century sat at the bottom of the pit.
7. The decision to cut spending on these social programs was painful and difficult.
9. If the legislation becomes law, it will have deep social effects.

Chapter 5

A.
1. fact; knows
3. fact
5. opinion; believed
7. fact
9. opinion; appears
11. fact
13. fact
15. opinion; likely

B.
1. the most significant
3. —————
5. quite elaborately
7. many problems; primarily
9. the most popular
11. the most dangerous
13. particularly valuable
15. should

C.
1. weak. SPE helps people to lose weight.
3. strong. Acid rain is destroying the maple trees of Canada and northern U.S.
5. strong. People are able to sleep at any time if the conditions are suitable and they choose to do so.
7. strong. Many people in industrialized countries have more dioxin in their tissues than is natural.
9. strong. Corporate managers tend to attach greater credibility to reports when these reports are in computer printout form than when they are typed — even when statements in the reports are completely absurd.

D.
1. yes
3. yes
5. no
7. no
9. no
11. yes
13. no
15. no

E.
1. yes
3. no
5. no
7. yes
9. yes
11. no
13. yes
15. yes
17. no
19. yes
21. yes
23. no
25. yes
27. yes
29. no

Chapter 6

A.
1. a; revive
3. c; tons
5. a; missed their families
7. a; childhood, later social behavior

9. c; regular intervals
B. 1a. mathematics
b. chemistry
3a. physics
b. electronics
5a. chemistry
b. medicine
c. physics
7a. geology
b. medicine
c. mathematics
9a. psychiatry
b. economics
c. meteorology
d. astronomy
C. 1. because
3. such as, for example
5. in the same way that
7. only
9. except for
11. in spite of
13. in whatever way
15. perhaps
17. simply
19. at that time
21. at one time
23. simply
25. but
27. approximation
29. synonymous expression
31. from the time of
33. consequently
35. quiet
37. after that
39. therefore
41. during the time that
43. up to this time
45. but
D. 1. l
3. o
5. c
7. i
9. f
11. g
13. n
15. k
E. 1. buying something, money, prices, business, etc.
3. Both are liquids and contain dissolved substances.
5. Both have an inner material between two outer layers of another material.
7. people; ears and mouths, etc.
9. rope
11. China was not economically active. It is like a giant in terms of both its great population and its size.
13. A person to lead them or to represent them.
15. Both of them flow.
F. 1. boiling water
3. a flower
5. a spider
7. a jet, rocket, bird
9. a highly infectious disease
G. 1. geology, geography, biography

    3.   thermometer, thermotropism, hydrotropism

Chapter 7

  A.   1. oscilloscope = instrument
        3. Polynesians = travelers
        5. contraption = gadget = contrivances
        7. automobiles = machines = vehicles
        9. container = vessel
  B.   1. it = sense of smell
        3. they = melting and boiling points
           this = the idea that the boiling points are constant
        5. its = Zuse's computer
           some = the descendants of Zuse's computer
        7. them = diseases
           these = cataracts
        9. he = Gaspard Monge
           he = Napoleon
           he = Gaspard Monge
           him = Napoleon
  C.   1. Different people have different needs, and these <u>needs</u> are often culturally-conditioned <u>needs</u>.
        3. The best <u>thing that</u> writers can do is hope <u>that</u> their work is widely read and understood.
        5. The average office worker in the U.S. rises at seven o'clock and at eight-thirty <u>o'clock the average office worker in the U.S.</u> steps into the car for the drive to work.
        7. The ordinary well is simply a hole <u>that is</u> dug or <u>a hole that is</u> drilled in an area where ground water is unconfirmed.
        9. All varieties of cheese are produced as a result of bacterial action, and many <u>varieties of cheese are produced</u> as a result of fungal action as well.
  D. 1a. that are
       b. land plants are
     3a. a
       b. a
       c. that is
       d. in
     5a. out of
       b. that are
       c. that are
       d. broad discipline
       e. that are
       f. that are
       g. broad discipline
       h. that are
       i. that is
  E.   1. Tokyo <u>to</u> Seattle

3. <u>from</u> 1929 <u>to</u> 1933
5. price <u>or</u> prices
7. Pages 52 <u>through</u> 58
9. synonyms
11. linguistic <u>and</u> or <u>or</u> sociological
13. first-in, first-out <u>abbreviated</u> as FIFO
15. Bello <u>from</u> U.S.A. and Hadjaj-Aoul <u>from</u> Algeria.

F.   1. et al; and others
3. etc.; and so on
5. e.g.; for example

Chapter 8

A.   1. false   11. true
3. false   13. true
5. true   15. true
7. false   17. false
9. true   19. true

B.   1. Answers will vary. Two methods are mining underground and panning sand and gravel found in rivers.
3. Answers will vary. The principal factor for the rise and fall of any commodity is the ratio between supply and demand. In the late 1970s, there was inflation in the United States which meant that dollars were losing their purchasing value while gold was perceived as retaining its value. As a result, the demand for gold was high. Five years later, the rate of inflation was markedly lower and there was less demand for gold.
5. Answers will vary. The word rand is from an Afrikaans word meaning shield. In Dutch, from which Afrikaans is derived, rand means edge or ridge. Witwatersrand is a ridge of gold-bearing rock 62 miles long and 23 miles wide in South Africa's Transvaal region. The government of South Africa named the currency of its country in honor of the ridge containing the precious metal that for many years was internationally recognized as the monetary standard.

C.   1. true   11. false   21. true   31. false   41. true
3. true   13. true   23. true   33. false   43. false
5. false   15. true   25. true   35. true   45. true
7. false   17. true   27. true   37. false   47. false
9. true   19. true   29. true   39. true   49. false

D.   1. Answers will vary depending on students' cultures.
3. Answers will vary. Some obvious places where the findings of the study might be applied are homes, offices, and classrooms.
5. Answers will vary. The red and green running lights of ships are one instance of internationally recognized colors. The white flag of truce is another.

E.   1. false   21. false   41. true   61. true
3. false   23. true   43. false   63. false
5. false   25. false   45. true   65. false
7. false   27. true   47. true   67. true
9. false   29. true   49. false   69. false

11.	true	31.	true	51.	false	71.	true
13.	false	33.	true	53.	true	73.	false
15.	true	35.	true	55.	true	75.	false
17.	false	37.	true	57.	true	77.	true
19.	true	39.	true	59.	true	79.	true

F. 1. Answers will vary. Iridium is found in great concentration in meteors and asteroids. It is also found in great concentration in the earth's core. Volcanoes release materials from the earth's core.

   3. Answers will vary. Clouds of dust might radically reduce sunlight and so stop the process of photosynthesis, which would stop the production of green plants, and destroy animals depending on them for food. This in turn would reduce the amount of food available to meat eaters. The clouds of dust might also radically reduce the temperature of the earth, killing heat-loving plants and animals and reducing the food supply for animals that ate them.

   5. Answers will vary. Following is a suggested flow chart.

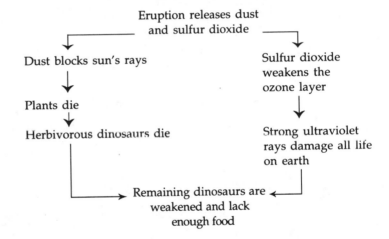

Index

Key: **boldfaced type** indicates the **page number(s)** where the entry is defined or discussed; **f** indicates that the entry is illustrated in a **figure**, and **t** indicates that the entry is illustrated in a **table**.